SING
TO THE
LORD

Also by Frank Colquhoun

A Hymn Companion
Parish Prayers
Contemporary Parish Prayers
New Parish Prayers

SING
TO THE
LORD

A Fresh Look at Some Favourite
Hymns of Praise

FRANK COLQUHOUN

Hodder & Stoughton

LONDON SYDNEY AUCKLAND TORONTO

British Library Cataloguing in Publication Data

Sing to the Lord.
  1. Christian church. Public worship.
  Hymns. Words –Anthologies
  I. Colquhoun, Frank
  264'.2

  ISBN 0-340-42691-8

To my friend

TIMOTHY DUDLEY-SMITH

with gratitude

FOREWORD

St Augustine defined a hymn as 'a song with praise to God' and commented, 'If you praise God and sing not, you utter no hymn. If you sing and praise not God, you utter no hymn. A hymn then contains these three things: song, and praise, and that of God.'

Songs of praise conform most nearly to this pattern. They are what hymns should truly be. For praise is of the very essence of Christian worship. It lifts our hearts to God and enables us to give him the honour due to his name.

But is there sufficient praise in our worship today? It was that question which suggested to me the writing of this book. Church services often tend to be too sombre and subjective, sometimes plain dull. The note of praise and joy is lacking and worshippers become occupied with themselves rather than with God.

This book therefore concentrates on hymns of praise. They are of widely different types. I have selected just over thirty, representing varied authors, dates, themes and styles. I hope that what I have written may help us to sing them with better understanding and so to rejoice in the Lord to the glory of his great name.

FRANK COLQUHOUN

CONTENTS
and Index of first lines

1

ALL HAIL THE POWER OF JESUS' NAME
Edward Perronet, 1726–92

'All hail the power of Jesus' name' is a universal hymn, known and sung the whole world over, yet it is not the work of a renowned hymn-writer. Edward Perronet did in fact write a great many hymns, but with this one exception they are now forgotten. Nevertheless, what a grand hymn by which to be remembered nearly two centuries later.

Let us begin by taking a look at the manner of man he was and the times in which he lived.

★　　★　　★

Edward Perronet was a member of a French Huguenot family and a product of the Evangelical Revival. His father, Vincent Perronet, vicar of Shoreham in Kent, was an intimate friend of John Wesley. Edward became one of Wesley's converts, and later was one of his first Methodist 'preachers' or ministers. Here he found an outlet for his spiritual gifts and evangelical zeal.

But not long afterwards he became disgruntled with the Church of England because as a layman he was not permitted to celebrate the holy communion. He published a bitter satire on the Church which deeply distressed the Wesley brothers. Eventually he parted company with them, turned Dissenter, and ended his days as minister of an Independent (Congregational) chapel in Canterbury.

It was during these later years that he wrote his 'Coronation' hymn as it has been called. The famous tune *Miles Lane* was composed for it at the same time by his friend William Shrubsole, a former chorister of Canterbury Cathedral, then aged only 19. Elgar pronounced it to be the finest English hymn tune ever written. The words with the music were published in 1780 in eight stanzas. Seven years later Dr John Rippon, a Baptist minister, included it in his *Selection of Hymns* with a number of alterations. These changes need not concern us now, for they do not affect the hymn's grand design, which is to affirm the kingship of Christ and to call upon various categories of creation to 'crown him Lord of all'.

★   ★   ★

These categories as I have called them determine the pattern of the hymn. First to be addressed are the angels.

> All hail the power of Jesus' name!
>   Let angels prostrate fall;
> Bring forth the royal diadem,
>   And crown him Lord of all.

The Bible is full of angels. So are the hymn-books. We shall meet with them again later on. Admittedly we do not know much about them, but they cannot be ignored or dismissed. The word 'angel' means a messenger, and in the capacity of God's messengers they repeatedly appear in the narratives of both Old and New Testaments. They evidently belong to an order of spiritual beings who worship God and serve his will in heaven, and minister to the heirs of salvation on earth (Heb. 1:14).

The hymn summons them to fall prostrate in homage to the Lord Jesus Christ and bring forth the royal diadem to crown him as the universal king. But his sovereignty is not only acknowledged in the spiritual sphere:

> Crown him, ye morning stars of light,
>   Who fixed this floating ball;

> Now hail the strength of Israel's might,
>   And crown him Lord of all.

The 'morning stars of light' (see Job 38:7) represent the world of nature, the material universe. All creation is to acknowledge Christ in his capacity as Creator; for 'all things were made by him, and without him was not anything made that was made' (John 1:3 AV). The poetic description of our planet as a 'floating ball' – floating yet fixed – is probably derived from Psalm 96:10: 'the world also shall be established that it shall not be moved' (AV).

We pass from the company of angels and the created order to the Church of God, beginning with the suffering Church.

> Crown him, ye martyrs of your God,
>   Who from his altar call;
> Extol the Stem-of-Jesse's rod,
>   And crown him Lord of all.

The martyrs are those who have borne their 'witness' (as the word means) to the utmost limit and died for the Faith. The Church has always honoured its martyrs. It has had them from the beginning and throughout the succeeding years. Perhaps the Church of this century has had more martyrs than that of any other age. The reference to the martyrs of God calling to him from his altar is borrowed from Revelation 6:9, 10.

★   ★   ★

To save space, and because it is slightly obscure, I am passing over the stanza 'Ye seed of Israel's race . . .' It appears to be addressed to Jewish Christians who, ransomed from their fallen state, owe their salvation to the grace of God, not to the law of Moses.

The stanza that follows has a wider perspective.

> Hail him, ye heirs of David's line,
> Whom David Lord did call,
> The God incarnate, Man divine,
> And crown him Lord of all.

Note carefully the lay-out of the stanza. The 'Hail him' is addressed to the 'heirs of David's line' – that is, to the whole people of God who by grace partake of David's royal character and are made 'kings and priests unto God' (Rev. 1:6 AV). And the one they are to hail is he whom David called 'Lord' – none other than Jesus Christ, 'the God incarnate, Man divine'.

This surely is the high point of the hymn. The person who as Christians we are to worship and enthrone is the Word made flesh, at once truly God and truly Man.

The previous stanzas have called upon specific companies to join in the coronation anthem: the angels, the created order, the martyrs, converted Jews and the Church of God. The next one is addressed simply to 'sinners' and this is where we come in.

> Sinners, whose love can ne'er forget
> The wormwood and the gall,
> Go, spread your trophies at his feet,
> And crown him Lord of all.

The words require little comment or explanation. The call now is not to sinners in general, but to redeemed sinners of every kind who acknowledge their indebtedness to Christ and 'whose love can ne'er forget the wormwood and the gall' – the bitter price paid for their redemption.

★   ★   ★

The final summons is to all mankind. It takes different forms in different books, but perhaps Dr Rippon's version is the most satisfactory:

> Let every kindred, every tribe,
>   On this terrestrial ball,
> To him all majesty ascribe,
>   And crown him Lord of all.

Whatever version is used, the meaning of the stanza remains the same. It is a call to the whole of humanity to acknowledge the kingship of Jesus and (in Perronet's original words) to 'shout in universal song' the praises of the Lord.

2

ALL PEOPLE THAT ON EARTH DO DWELL
William Kethe, d. 1594

This may not be the greatest hymn of praise in the English language, but it is certainly the oldest. It was published in London in 1561, shortly after Queen Elizabeth came to the throne, which means that it has been in unbroken use for more than 400 years. It is interesting to reflect that the famous words and the equally famous tune were doubt-less familiar to William Shakespeare and to other great Elizabethans.

★   ★   ★

For its origin therefore we have to go back a long way in history: to the stormy days of the Reformation and in particular to the reign of Queen Mary (1553–8). For English Protestants it was a reign of terror. Many devout Christians who refused to submit to the Church of Rome were persecuted, imprisoned or put to death.

Those who could do so sought refuge on the Continent until the Queen's death enabled them to return to England. Among them was William Kethe, the author of this hymn. He was of Scottish birth, but was ordained in the Church of England. In 1555 he went into exile in Germany, but later moved to Geneva. This brought him into touch with John Calvin and a group of scholars who were engaged in translating the Bible into English. Kethe, an erudite man, had an important share in this work which when completed became known as the Genevan Bible.

What is more to our purpose, he also assisted in the task of producing a complete English version of the metrical psalms. He himself contributed twenty-five psalms to the book, published in 1561 as the Anglo-Genevan Psalter; and it is from this source that 'All people that on earth do dwell' is derived.

The hymn is a rendering of the one hundredth psalm, commonly known as the *Jubilate Deo* from its first words in the Latin. It was set to a tune by the Frenchman Louis Bourgeois (born about 1510) and now known as the *Old Hundredth*.

Two facts are worth noting here. The first is that throughout the centuries the hymn has never been sung to any other than its original tune. Perhaps even more remarkable is the fact that the hymn has remained unchanged from the beginning. It has mercifully escaped the treatment of editors who have a habit of revising and 'improving' hymns, especially old ones. We sing it today almost exactly as William Kethe wrote it.

★   ★   ★

In the Authorised Version of the Bible (which I shall quote throughout this chapter) Psalm 100 begins: 'Make a joyful noise unto the Lord, all ye lands'. Kethe renders this:

> All people that on earth do dwell,
>   Sing to the Lord with cheerful voice.

Note how 'all lands' becomes 'all people', which is more personal. But in either case the invitation is universal. It calls on the whole population of the world wherever they live to join in the worship of Jehovah.

The psalm continues: 'Serve the Lord with gladness: comes before his presence with singing'. This becomes:

Him serve with fear, his praise forthtell,
　　Come ye before him and rejoice.

Here we meet with another difference between the two
versions, this time of more importance. 'Serve the Lord
with gladness,' says the psalm. 'Serve him with fear,' writes
Kethe, somewhat strangely. Gladness and fear do not correspond, even granting that fear means reverence. For this
reason the *Scottish Psalter* of 1650 altered the third line to
'Serve him with mirth, his praise forthtell,' a rendering
which several hymnals have since adopted. Our religion
could do with a bit more mirth or merriment, as the word
means.

★　　★　　★

'Know ye that the Lord he is God: it is he that hath made us,
and not we ourselves; we are his people, and the sheep of
his pasture'. So the psalm, verse 3. The margin gives an
alternative rendering of 'and not we ourselves', namely 'and
we are his'. This is adopted in all modern translations of the
psalm and also by Kethe:

　　The Lord ye know is God indeed;
　　　Without our aid he did us make;
　　We are his folk, he doth us feed,
　　　And for his sheep he doth us take.

'We are his folk' – that is, his people. We belong to him and
he takes care of his own. And we are not only his *folk*: we are
also his *flock*. The two words are much alike and in early
versions of the hymn they were sometimes confused. In
keeping with the psalm Kethe wrote, 'And for his sheep he
doth us take.'

　　What then? Calvin comments here: 'Seeing that the Lord
ceases not to deal with us in this manner, it would be more
than a shame to grow weary in offering him our praise.'
Accordingly the hymn continues:

> O enter then his gates with praise,
>   Approach with joy his courts unto;
> Praise, laud and bless his name always,
>   For it is seemly so to do.

This echoes the words of the psalm, 'Enter into his gates with thanksgiving, and into his courts with praise: be thankful unto him, and bless his name.'

Do not fail to note the significance of these words. The *gates* referred to are the temple gates in Jerusalem; the *courts* are the temple courts. And the invitation is still universal, addressed to 'all people that on earth do dwell'.

The psalmist catches a marvellous vision. He sees people of every race and nation surging into the Jewish sanctuary amid songs of praise and thanksgiving. There is no longer a court of the Gentiles. The temple has become, as God intended it to be, a house of prayer for all nations. At this point the psalm becomes a prophecy of the Messianic age and the hymn strikes a missionary note.

★   ★   ★

The expression 'For why' at the beginning of the fourth stanza means 'because' and gives the reason for praising God.

> For why the Lord our God is good,
>   His mercy is for ever sure;
> His truth at all times firmly stood,
>   And shall from age to age endure.

This is Kethe's rendering of: 'For the Lord is good, his mercy is everlasting; and his truth endureth to all generations.'

In this its final verse another element enters the psalm, the element of eternity or timelessness. God's mercy is everlasting. His truth (or faithfulness) endures to all generations. So as the psalm begins by broadening our horizon, it ends by lengthening our view.

This is superbly expressed by Isaac Watts in the last stanza of his paraphrase of the psalm, beginning 'Before Jehovah's aweful throne':

> Wide as the world is thy command,
>   Vast as eternity thy love;
> Firm as a rock thy truth shall stand,
>   When rolling years shall cease to move.

3

ALLELUIA! SING TO JESUS
W. Chatterton Dix, 1837–98

The author of this hymn was a devout Anglican layman, William Chatterton Dix, the son of a Bristol surgeon. Instead of following in his father's footsteps he chose a career in the world of commerce and for many years was manager of a marine insurance company in Glasgow.

An incident that happened during those years is worth recording. Glasgow was a busy port with ships sailing to all parts of the world. The insurance of the vessels, their passengers and cargo, was of utmost importance in days when sea travel was still a hazardous affair.

A ship bound for New Zealand seemed to have been lost, for her return to port was long overdue. When hope was almost abandoned Dix remembered that shortly before the ship sailed her captain, a Christian, had called at his office to sign the policy and had then remarked that in faith he had committed the voyage into God's hands.

On recalling this Dix felt reassured, and a day or two later the ship was sighted and safely docked amid the rejoicings of a big crowd. Then someone caught sight of Dix – not joining in the shouting and singing, but quietly kneeling in prayer, thanking God for the ship's return and for honouring the captain's faith.

★　　★　　★

Such was the man who wrote this hymn. He was also the author of the popular Epiphany hymn, 'As with gladness men of old' and the harvest hymn, 'To thee, O Lord, our hearts we raise'.

He wrote 'Alleluia! sing to Jesus' as a communion hymn for the feast of the Ascension. This is a point worth noting. It is not a general hymn of praise for all occasions, but a hymn in which two distinct themes are blended, the Eucharist and the Ascension.

Another thing to note is the recurrence of the word *Alleluia*. The hymn begins with it, as does every stanza. The word is derived from the Jewish psalter and means 'Praise the Lord!' It early passed into the worship of the Christian Church, partly from its use in Revelation 19:6: 'Alleluia! For the Lord our God the Almighty reigns.'

> Alleluia! sing to Jesus!
>   His the sceptre, his the throne;
> Alleluia! his the triumph,
>   His the victory alone;
> Hark! the songs of peaceful Sion
>   Thunder like a mighty flood;
> Jesus out of every nation
>   Hath redeemed us by his blood.

Dix entitled his hymn, 'Redemption through the Precious Blood' and quoted as a text Revelation 5:9: 'And they sung a new song, saying Thou art worthy . . . for thou wast slain, and hast redeemed us to God by thy blood out of every kindred, and tongue, and people, and nation' (AV). Against that background we get a clearer understanding of this stanza.

The first note it sounds is praise and glory to the ascended Lord Jesus. He is the king: the sceptre and the throne are his. He is also the conqueror, triumphant over every foe; and by his cross and passion he is the Redeemer of all mankind.

This magnificent portrayal of Christ in his heavenly glory makes an arresting start to the hymn. It continues:

> Alleluia! not as orphans
>   Are we left in sorrow now;
> Alleluia! he is near us,

Faith believes, nor questions how;
Though the cloud from sight received him
When the forty days were o'er,
Shall our hearts forget his promise,
'I am with you evermore'?

This, as we have said, is a sacramental hymn; but the second stanza reminds us that it is not only in the communion service that we enjoy the presence of Christ, nor does his bodily ascension into heaven separate him from us now. His 'Lo, I am with you always' means what it says. Before his passion he promised his disciples, 'I will not leave you comfortless. I will come to you' (John 14:18 AV). And he came to them in the power of the Spirit at Pentecost, to abide with his Church for evermore.

The Holy Spirit is Christ in us. It is important to remember that the Holy Spirit was given not to compensate for Christ's absence but to ensure his presence. What *we* need above all is to realise and practise his presence at all times in our daily lives.

★   ★   ★

The third stanza begins with a reference to the Eucharist.

Alleluia! Bread of angels,
Thou on earth our food, our stay;
Alleluia! here the sinful
Flee to thee from day to day;
Intercessor, Friend of sinners,
Earth's Redeemer, plead for me,
Where the songs of all the sinless
Sweep across the crystal sea.

Jesus is the 'Bread of angels'. The expression is a reference to the manna from heaven in Psalm 78:25 ('men ate the bread of angels'), now applied to Jesus the true bread from heaven (John 6:32). He is our food as well as our 'stay' or strength.

Other descriptive titles follow. Jesus is our *Intercessor* who represents us to the Father and pleads our cause. He is the *Friend of sinners*, a name flung at him in derision by his enemies, but for all that gloriously true (Matt. 11:19). And it is true because he is the world's *Redeemer*, the slain lamb, who came to this earth to die for sinners.

All this gives us food for thought. And there is more to think about on the same lines in the final stanza.

> Alleluia! King eternal,
>   Thee the Lord of lords we own;
> Alleluia! born of Mary,
>   Earth thy footstool, heaven thy throne;
> Thou within the veil hast entered,
>   Robed in flesh, our great High Priest;
> Thou on earth both priest and victim,
>   In the eucharistic feast.

'King eternal' is a title which recognises the royalty of Jesus, as does also 'Lord of lords' (Rev. 19:16). While earth is his footstool, heaven is his throne. The point is that the incarnate Son now *reigns*.

In the final words the two themes of the Ascension and the Eucharist are combined. Having passed through the veil into the presence of God he is now our great High Priest. On earth, in the sacramental feast, he is both priest and victim. He is the priest (not High Priest, note) who still presides at the table as he did on the night of the institution. He is the victim whose perfect and all-sufficient sacrifice we celebrate in the broken bread and outpoured wine.

Alleluia!

4

AND CAN IT BE THAT I SHOULD GAIN
Charles Wesley, 1707–88

This favourite Methodist hymn is usually associated, and rightly so, with Charles Wesley's conversion which took place on Whitsunday, 1738. It was the turning-point in his life, though he had been a deeply religious man long before. Indeed, his conversion is a warning to church people that it is not enough to be religious, moral and orthodox. Wesley was all these things before his conversion. An ordained priest of the Church of England, he was devout and full of good works; but something was lacking, and he knew it.

What happened on that memorable Sunday was an *evangelical* conversion: that is, he personally experienced the saving truth of the gospel. He *knew* the gospel well, of course, and believed every word of it, but he had never known its power in his life. Then in God's mercy the transforming event took place.

At the time, far from well and restless in spirit, he was encouraged by a friend to study Luther's commentary on the Epistle to the Galatians. In doing so he was arrested by St Paul's words, 'The Son of God who loved me, and gave himself for me' (2:20). Luther emphasised the importance of the personal pronouns. 'Lay hold on the little word *me* with a sure faith,' he wrote, 'and apply it to yourself.' Wesley accepted Luther's counsel. In a flash he saw the necessity of a personal faith and the sufficiency of Christ's sacrifice, and he found all joy and peace in believing.

*　　*　　*

With his conversion began Wesley's great outburst of spiritual song. His vast mass of hymns all date from that event – a quite remarkable fact. 'And can it be' was one of his first hymns, written in the glow of his conversion experience. If you look at it in that light you will gain a deeper insight into its meaning.

> And can it be that I should gain
>   An interest in the Saviour's blood?
> Died he for me, who caused his pain,
>   For me, who him to death pursued?
> Amazing love! how can it be
> That thou, my God, shouldst die for me?

Not surprisingly Wesley begins his hymn on a note of wonder. He can hardly get over the astonishing thing that has happened to him. It was a miracle of grace. 'Can it possibly be true?' he is asking. 'Did Christ really die *for me*?' Those two words occur three times in the stanza and in a sense they are the key to the entire hymn.

He entitled his hymn 'Free Grace'. Before, he had been trusting in his merits, his religious works, his own efforts to please God. Now he had grasped hold of the *grace* of God, his 'amazing love', free, unmerited, unlimited: his love for all sinners, and most wonderful of all for *him*. If there is one thing that Wesley's experience teaches us it is that religion only becomes real when it becomes personal.

In the next stanza Wesley dwells further on the grace of God and illustrates it from the Incarnation.

> He left his Father's throne above –
>   So free, so infinite his grace! –
> Emptied himself of all but love,
>   And bled for Adam's helpless race.
> 'Tis mercy all, immense and free,
> For, O my God, it found out me!

Wesley was both a theologian and a Bible scholar. Here we see him in both capacities. His teaching on the Incarnation is based on a famous New Testament passage, Philippians 2:5–11. When Jesus 'left his Father's throne above' and became Man, the Scripture (RSV) says, literally, 'he *emptied* himself'; not of course of his deity, for that was impossible. He emptied himself of his heavenly glory in order to share our humanity. But of one thing, Wesley insists, he did not empty himself: his love for sinners, the love that was demonstrated by his becoming 'obedient unto death, even the death of the cross'. And at the thought of this the poet cries out with deep emotion,

> 'Tis mercy all, immense and free,
> For, O my God, it found out me!

*   *   *

What shall we say of the next stanza? Surely at this point the hymn reaches its loftiest height. The words are not only a vivid illustration of Wesley's conversion experience, they are also a fine example of his poetic power.

> Long my imprisoned spirit lay
>   Fast bound in sin and nature's night;
> Thine eye diffused a quickening ray –
>   I woke, the dungeon flamed with light;
> My chains fell off, my heart was free,
> I rose, went forth, and followed thee.

Clearly the picture here is drawn from the account of Peter's miraculous release from prison in Acts 12:6–9. Peter was under sentence of death. On the night before his execution he was sleeping in his cell, bound by two chains. Suddenly the angel of the Lord appeared and a light shone in the cell. He awoke Peter, saying, 'Get up quickly.' At once the chains fell off, the prison door opened, and he went forth a free man.

In dramatic and vivid verse Wesley puts himself in the place of the apostle. *He* is the prisoner, bound by his sins and all is dark. Then by the grace of God he is awakened to his need and the gospel light shines upon him. He is released from his bondage and his heart is free to follow Christ.

Wesley interprets his conversion as a divine act of deliverance. 'Christ has set us free!' cries St Paul – free from the bondage of sin, the condemnation of the law, the fear of death. The saving experience had other meanings for Wesley as well, as the final stanza discloses.

> No condemnation now I dread:
>   Jesus, and all in him, is mine!
> Alive in him, my living Head,
>   And clothed in righteousness divine.
> Bold I approach the eternal throne,
> And claim the crown, through Christ, my own.

'Jesus, and all in him, is mine' (see, 1 Cor. 3:22, 23). And what does that *all* include? The new life in Christ (Eph. 2:4, 5); the righteousness of God through faith (Phil. 3:9), free access to the throne of grace (Heb. 4:16), and the crown of glory hereafter (2 Tim. 4:8).

Evidently this hymn by his brother Charles was dear to John Wesley. On the last Sunday afternoon of his life when, very weak in body, he was asked by a friend whether his faith was the same as ever, he replied firmly, 'Yes' and then repeated the lines:

> Bold I approach the eternal throne,
> And claim the crown, through Christ, my own.

5

ANGEL VOICES EVER SINGING
Francis Pott, 1832–1909

This hymn has an unusual history. It owes its existence to the enterprise of a country parson more than a hundred years ago. He was the Rev. W.K. Macrorie, vicar of Wingates, a small and obscure parish in Lancashire. A new organ was to be installed in the village church and he was planning a suitable dedication service.

It was hardly a very auspicious occasion, but he felt a new hymn would be appropriate; so he boldly approached the Rev. Francis Pott, one of the editors of *Hymns Ancient and Modern*, and asked if he would write one for the service. To his delight – and perhaps to his surprise – his request was granted and 'Angel voices ever singing' came into being.

Having so far succeeded he went a step further and wrote to Dr E.G. Monk, a leading church musician and composer of the day, in the hope that he would provide music to match the words. Again he met with a favourable response and the fine tune *Angel Voices* was written for the hymn, first sung in Wingates Church in 1861. Words and music have remained wedded ever since. It is an ideal hymn for choir festivals and the like.

★　　★　　★

Angel voices ever singing
    Round thy throne of light,
Angel harps for ever ringing,
    Rest not day nor night;

> Thousands only live to bless thee
>   And confess thee
>   Lord of might.

The general theme of the hymn is the Church's worship, and it begins on this high note by reminding us of the worship offered to God in heaven. There, angels are the singers who with their harps surround 'the throne of light' and ceaselessly make music to the Lord. Doubtless Francis Pott was thinking of some words in the book of Revelation 14:2,3: 'I heard a voice from heaven like the sound of many waters and like the sound of loud thunder; the voice I heard was like the sound of harpists playing on their harps, and they sang a new song before the throne.'

In the Bible, heaven is envisaged as a very musical place. It is something like a great choral society with orchestral accompaniment. Not only are the voices of angels singing God's praise, but there is heard also the sound of harpists and minstrels, of flute players and trumpeters (Rev. 18:22).

This fact forms the background of the hymn, which next raises a question:

> Thou who art beyond the farthest
>   Mortal eye can scan,
> Can it be that thou regardest
>   Songs of sinful man?
> Can we know that thou art near us,
>   And wilt hear us?
>   Yea, we can.

The question is a pertinent one. God is transcendent, far above us in his infinite glory. It may well be that he is delighted with the songs of angels and the celestial host; but is it possible that he has any regard for 'the songs of sinful man' here on earth? Can we dare to believe that he is actually near and not far off, that he will listen to *our* praises as well as to those of the angels?

'Yes, we can!' is the reassuring answer. The transcendence of God, which we acknowledge every time we address him as 'Our Father *in heaven*,' does not cut him off from us. He is still our Father, who loves us and all his children and is pleased to accept what they have to offer him.

★   ★   ★

This is the theme of the next stanza:

> Yea, we know that thou rejoicest
>   O'er each work of thine;
> Thou didst ears and hands and voices
>   For thy praise design;
> Craftsman's art and music's measure
>   For thy pleasure
>   All combine.

In these words we have a direct allusion to the dedication service for which the hymn was written. God rejoices in all the works of men designed for his praise. Those works involve the use of their 'ears and hands and voices'. How is this so?

Christian worship is a response to the Word of God which we hear with our *ears*. It expresses itself among other things in the playing of musical instruments with our *hands*, as likewise in the lifting up of our *voices* in 'psalms and hymns and spiritual songs'.

The words 'craftsman's art' are clearly a reference to the new organ to be dedicated. Those who know anything about organ-building will agree that it represents a very high degree of craftsmanship, even if it is only for a small instrument. And 'music's measure' describes the choral part of the service and the organist's voluntary, not forgetting of course the singing of our hymn.

The verse that follows also has that occasion in mind.

In thy house, great God, we offer
  Of thine own to thee;
And for thine acceptance proffer
  All unworthily
Hearts and minds and hands and voices
  In our choicest
    Psalmody.

There is quite a lot to think about in these words. For one thing they remind us that we can only offer to God what is rightly his own – his, not ours. Again, our worship, even at its best, is unworthy of him, far less than the honour due to his name. And again, we recognise that worship demands a lot from us and involves the use of all our faculties: 'hearts and minds and hands and voices'.

*   *   *

In these reflections we have related the hymn to what happened in a small village church when it was first sung many years ago. But we must also relate it to our own worship and what goes on in our churches Sunday by Sunday. Worship is something that involves us all. We are present in church not as spectators but as participants. We have to *give* as well as to receive. And all that we offer to God must be for *his* glory, not our own or that of the choir or organist or anybody else.

As if to drive that home the hymn fittingly ends on this high note:

Honour, glory, might, and merit
  Thine shall ever be,
Father, Son, and Holy Spirit,
  Blessed Trinity!
Of the best that thou hast given
  Earth and heaven
    Render thee.

6

BRIGHT THE VISION THAT DELIGHTED
Richard Mant, 1776–1848

Here is a hymn which carries us in thought to the city of Jerusalem more than two and a half thousand years ago. That accounts for the somewhat obscure allusions in the opening stanza to a bright vision and someone described as Judah's seer.

All this becomes clear once we recognise the hymn's Biblical setting, Isaiah 6:1–3. That passage provides the key to it all. But first a word about the hymn's author.

⋆　　⋆　　⋆

Perhaps the chief thing to be said about Richard Mant is that he was a very scholarly man. Educated at Winchester and Oxford, he was ordained in 1802 and served a number of parishes until finally he became rector of St Botolph's, Bishopsgate, London. Then his ministry switched from England to Ireland when at the age of 40 he was consecrated Bishop of Killarie, and soon after moved to the see of Down and Connor.

It seems that his episcopate gave him more scope for writing, as in the succeeding years he produced a number of books, including a collection of hymns. Many of these were translations from the medieval Latin services. Of his own hymns only two or three are still in use; but among them is 'Bright the vision', and that one hymn is probably worth more than all the others.

⋆　　⋆　　⋆

The hymn was written for Trinity Sunday and entitled 'Commemoration of the Thrice Holy'. So we come to the words of Scripture on which it is based, a very familiar Old Testament passage:

> In the year that King Uzziah died I saw also the Lord sitting upon a throne, high and lifted up, and his train filled the temple. Above it stood the seraphim: each one had six wings; with twain he covered his face, and with twain he covered his feet, and with twain he did fly. And one cried unto another and said, Holy, holy, holy, is the Lord of hosts: the whole earth is full of his glory (Isa. 6:1–3 AV).

Here in imagination we are in the ancient city of Jerusalem. The year is 740 BC, the year that King Uzziah died. Isaiah, then a young man, enters the temple to worship. Doubtless he had done the same many times before. But on this never-to-be-forgotten occasion something extraordinary happens which changes the whole current of his life. He meets with the living God and receives his commission to be a prophet to Israel.

The opening words of the hymn recount his experience.

> Bright the vision that delighted
>   Once the sight of Judah's seer;
> Sweet the countless tongues united
>   To entrance the prophet's ear.

Here is the 'bright vision' that the young Isaiah saw. And what a vision it was! He saw the Lord 'sitting upon a throne, high and lifted up'. It was a vision of the majesty of God, God in his transcendent glory. The hymn says the sight 'delighted' the prophet. But is that right? The Bible declares that he was entirely overwhelmed by what he saw. '. . . my eyes have seen the King, the Lord of hosts', he cried. And that vision of God enabled him to see himself as he really was, a man of unclean lips, quite unfit to be a prophet of the Lord without the cleansing fire.

But this stanza is concerned not only with what Isaiah saw that day. It is concerned also with what he heard, the sound of countless voices united in singing God's praise. The second stanza identifies the singers:

> Round the Lord in glory seated,
>   Cherubim and Seraphim
> Filled his temple, and repeated
>   Each to each the alternate hymn.

The majestic scene is here further described. The Bible account says the cherubim and seraphim stood *above* the throne. The hymn describes them as seated *round* the Lord. The difference is slight, but there is something to be said for the alteration, for now the Lord is at the centre of worship, as he must always be. The reference to the throne reminds us again of his sovereignty.

The cherubim and seraphim belong to the highest order of angelic beings, devoted to the service and worship of God. They are heard singing one to another 'the alternate hymn':

> 'Lord, thy glory fills the heaven,
>   Earth is with its fullness stored;
> Unto thee be glory given,
>   Holy, holy, holy, Lord'

This angelic song is also heard in the New Testament. The heavenly host around the throne of God chant endlessly, 'Holy, holy, holy, is the Lord God Almighty, who was, and is, and is to come' (Rev. 4:8). The *Ter Sanctus* ('holy, holy, holy' as it is called) has been part of the worship of the Christian Church from at least the fourth century and is still sung in the communion service:

> Holy, holy, holy, Lord, God of power and might,
> Heaven and earth are full of your glory,
>   Hosanna in the highest.

The song is a pure act of adoration and compels us to think of the *holiness* of God. Perhaps we do not think of that enough. God is love, as we all recognise. But God is also holy. He is Holy Love. This is the essence of his being.

✦   ✦   ✦

> Heaven is still with glory ringing,
>   Earth takes up the angels' cry,
> 'Holy, holy, holy,' singing,
>   'Lord of hosts, the Lord most high.'

The hymn here reminds us that the song of the angels in heaven finds its echo in the songs of the Church on earth. And the stanza that follows links these two together:

> With his seraph train before him,
>   With his holy Church below,
> Thus unite we to adore him,
>   Bid we thus our anthems flow.

The value of this stanza is that it brings *us* into the action. Note the personal pronouns and the reference to God's 'holy Church'. Of that company we ourselves are all members, and as a result 'thus *unite we* to adore him' with the whole Church in earth and heaven:

> 'Lord, thy glory fills the heaven;
>   Earth is with its fullness stored;
> Unto thee be glory given,
>   Holy, holy, holy, Lord.'

7

CHRIST IS THE KING! O FRIENDS REJOICE
G.K.A. Bell, 1883–1958

Strictly speaking, of course, this is not a hymn of praise; but it is infused with the spirit of praise and sparkles with Alleluias. That apart, it seemed good to include the hymn because of its distinctive character. It deals with the important subject of Christian unity and was written by one of the great English churchmen of this century who did so much to promote that unity.

*　　*　　*

George Kennedy Allen Bell was the son of a clergyman who after his ordination in 1907 was in turn a curate at Leeds, an Oxford don, and chaplain to Archbishop Davidson. In 1924 he became Dean of Canterbury and four years later was consecrated Bishop of Chichester. Throughout his ministry he threw himself wholeheartedly into the ecumenical movement and in later life was President of the World Council of Churches.

Before the war he had established close relations with the oppressed Church in Hitler's Germany, particularly with the Lutheran pastor Dietrich Bonhoeffer. This continued as far as possible during the war years. He made it clear that he had no hatred of the German people, only of the evil Nazi régime. Indeed, he had a deep compassion for the Germans' sufferings and with great courage protested in the name of God against the Allies' indiscriminate bombing of German cities.

This brought him into disfavour with the high-ups in the British government who suspected him of being pro-German. It is now generally accepted that it was because of this that he was passed over as Archbishop of Canterbury in 1944 on the death of William Temple. He put God before State and paid the price accordingly. His memory is still honoured in the German Lutheran Church.

★   ★   ★

So we come to George Bell's hymn, first published in 1931.

> Christ is the King! O friends rejoice;
> Brothers and sisters, with one voice
> Make all men know he is your choice.
> *Alleluia.*

The hymn opens with a bold affirmation of the sovereignty of Christ, and this is the keynote throughout. All that it has to say about the Church – past, present, or future – is based on the fact that Christ's reign or kingdom extends over all.

Next comes a call to Christians to recognise that fact and rejoice. They are addressed as 'friends'; but they are more than friends, as the next line makes clear by calling them 'brothers and sisters'. That is something quite different and something that has a direct bearing on the theme of Christian unity.

If believers are indeed brothers and sisters they are all children of the same Father and members of the same family. In the deepest sense they are already one in Christ. This is the basic unity we affirm whenever we say 'Our Father'. We are bound together not simply by friendship but by spiritual kinship. Shortly before he died Bonhoeffer sent this verbal message to Bishop Bell: 'Tell him that, with him, I believe in the principle of our universal Christian brotherhood which rises above all national interests.'

The hymn accordingly continues on the note of praise.

> O magnify the Lord, and raise
> Anthems of joy and holy praise
> For Christ's brave saints of ancient days.

Who were these brave saints? I think it is clear from what follows that they were the saints of the New Testament Church: its apostles, prophets, teachers, and perhaps especially its martyrs. We need constantly to honour their lives, sufferings and sacrifices; and incidentally this is one of the values of observing Saints' Days.

So it is good that at this point the hymn looks back to the Church's past. We should certainly do the same from time to time, for while it is a bad thing for Christians to *live* in the past, they can assuredly *learn* from the past, particularly from the heroic example of Christ's disciples of old.

*   *   *

> They with a faith for ever new
> Followed the King, and round him drew
> Thousands of faithful men and true.

The words of this stanza are the Acts of the Apostles in miniature. They call for no comment, but note one simple point. The early witnesses for Christ their King drew thousands of faithful disciples round him. Yes, round *him*, not round themselves. It was a tragedy when members of the Corinthian Church began saying 'I am of Paul' or 'I am of Apollos', seemingly drawn to their leaders rather than to their Lord.

The next stanza moves out of the past into the present and in a sense links them together.

> O Christian women, Christian men,
> All the world over, seek again
> The Way disciples followed then.

The Church of today does not need a new faith. What it needs is to adhere to the old faith, 'the Way disciples followed then'. That is an interesting phrase, *the Way*. Possibly it refers simply to Christ himself, the one and only Way to the Father (John 14:6). But the phrase is also used in the New Testament as a description of the Christian religion as a whole (Acts 9:2, etc.) and suggests among other things that Christianity is a pilgrim's path which leads from this world to the next.

Where do *we* come in all this? Here is the answer.

> Christ through all ages is the same:
> Place the same hope in his great name,
> With the same faith his word proclaim.

There is a challenge for us all here, and it is found in the threefold recurrence of the word *same*. It challenges us, first, to be loyal to the same *Christ*, the eternal, unchanging Son of God. Second, to place the same *hope* in him as did his first disciples. And third, to proclaim the gospel with the same *faith* as theirs.

> Let Love's unconquerable might
> Your scattered companies unite
> In service to the Lord of light.

Here is a further challenge in 'Love's unconquerable might'. It is Love with a capital 'L' you will note, Christ's love, not ours. It is his love alone that has the power to break down the barriers and unite our 'scattered companies' – an apt description still of much of our church life. So we dare not be complacent. The whole point of Bishop Bell's hymn is to awaken us from our lethargy, to remind us of Christ's plan for his Church, and rekindle our faith and love as we face the future.

So shall God's will on earth be done,
New lamps be lit, new tasks begun,
And the whole Church at last be one.
Alleluia.

8

COME, WE THAT LOVE THE LORD
Isaac Watts, 1674–1748

Many hymns are not as well known in the Church of
England as they are in the Free Churches. This one is an
example. To the majority of Anglicans it is probably a 'new'
hymn, but Nonconformists in general will be familiar with
it.

Its author was the great Dr Isaac Watts, rightly known as
the father of English hymnody. It was he who in his early
life courageously broke the long tradition of using only
metrical psalms in Christian worship and began writing
hymns. These at once became popular among Dissenters
and paved the way for Charles Wesley a generation later.
Apart from his 600 or so hymns Isaac Watts was a distinguished minister and scholar: Edinburgh University
conferred on him the degree of Doctor of Divinity.

★　　★　　★

This hymn comes from his *Hymns and Spiritual Songs*, 1707.
It was headed 'Heavenly Joy on Earth', and this is the
hymn's dominant theme. It begins with an invitation.

> Come, we that love the Lord,
>   And let our joys be known;
> Join in a song with sweet accord,
>   And thus surround the Throne.

You will see that the invitation is not of a general character.
It is addressed specifically to Christians, to those who love
the Lord; and it urges them to let their joys be known.

What are those joys? As the theme of Christian joy runs throughout the hymn we ought to be clear about this. Christian joy is essentially spiritual in character: inward, not outward. It is quite different from human happiness or merriment, or having a good time. It is the joy of which Christ is the source and substance, the joy of forgiveness, reconciliation, freedom, victory, life eternal; the joy of daily fellowship with God, the joy of knowing him, trusting him, serving him. All this is 'spiritual', and because it is that no one can take it from us.

This joy finds its expression in song which those who love the Lord sing with 'one accord' and which surrounds the throne of God in heaven.

The stanza that follows is omitted in some hymn-books.

> The sorrows of the mind
> Be banished from the place!
> Religion never was designed
> To make our pleasures less.

By 'the sorrows of the mind' Watts seems to mean gloomy thoughts; and by the 'place' he is probably referring to the place of worship, or possibly the place where we live. Gloom should be banished from both, for both should be places of holy joy.

Watts expresses a wholesome truth when he says: 'Religion never was designed to make our pleasures less' – words worthy of a place in the *Oxford Dictionary of Quotations*. It is a truth that needs to be affirmed again and again, for far from diminishing the healthy pleasures of life the Christian religion increases and enriches them.

★   ★   ★

Watts pursues his theme:

> Let those refuse to sing
> Who never knew our God,

But servants of the heavenly King
May speak their joys abroad.

Those who 'never knew our God' – that is, the godless and unconverted – have every cause for refusing to sing, for they have nothing to sing about apart from the trivial, temporal things of earth. There is some truth in the saying that Christians are the only people who have a right to be happy, for as 'servants of the heavenly King' they possess heavenly joys. Watts wants to dispel the illusion that Christians are either joyless or joy-killers.

Another stanza puts it like this:

The men of grace have found
Glory begun below,
Celestial fruits on earthly ground
From faith and hope may grow.

Here we come to the hymn's main theme, 'Heavenly joys on earth'. The language abounds in splendid phrases. Believers are 'men [and women] of grace', for it is by the grace of God, his free, boundless, unmerited love, that they are what they are (*cf.* 1 Cor. 15:10).

Again, heaven is not only above us and beyond us. It is within us, 'glory begun below'. Heaven begins in what we are *now*. The 'celestial fruits' grown on 'earthly ground' through the exercise of faith and hope.

And more in the same strain follows:

The hill of Zion yields
A thousand sacred sweets,
Before we reach the heavenly fields,
Or walk the golden streets.

The design of the gospel is not simply to transport us at last to heaven. It is also to make earth more like heaven and give us a foretaste of it. Before we 'walk the golden streets' we can experience something of the heavenly life in the worship and fellowship of the Church, if the Church is anything like it ought to be.

*   *   *

>   Yes, and before we rise
>   To that immortal state,
>   The thoughts of such amazing bliss
>   Should constant joys create.

In the course of our mundane, earthbound lives do we *think* sufficiently of heaven? Clearly we should not always be thinking of it, but that is very different from never doing so, except perhaps in church on Sundays. Our hymns are full of heaven, and perhaps one of their spiritual values is to remind us of the glorious goal of our pilgrimage and to teach us to sing with joy as we go on our way.

On that cheerful note Watts ends his hymn:

>   Then let our songs abound,
>   And every tear be dry;
>   We're marching through Immanuel's ground
>   To fairer worlds on high.

9

CROWN HIM WITH MANY CROWNS
Matthew Bridges, 1800–94, and
Godfrey Thring, 1823–1903

This hymn finds a place in almost every hymnal, but not always in the same form. As a matter of interest I looked it up in seven well-known books and in every case the versions differed in some way.

Of course, this puzzling fact is not of much concern to the average worshipper who simply sings the hymn in the words provided. All the same, the puzzling fact calls for some explanation, and the twofold authorship of the hymn provides the key. The original author was Matthew Bridges, an Anglican layman who at the age of 48 became a Roman Catholic. His hymn, consisting of six verses, appeared three years later in his *Hymns of the Heart*.

The other author, Godfrey Thring, was a prebendary of Wells Cathedral. He was attracted by Bridges' work and in 1880 produced a new and – doubtless what he considered to be – an improved version of the hymn. He borrowed, with permission, the original opening stanza and then added others of his own. The outcome was that hymn-book editors were confronted with a choice of material and put together their own versions. This explains why our hymnals differ. But it must be added that both *Ancient and Modern* and the *English Hymnal* use only the work of Matthew Bridges.

★   ★   ★

All this is pretty dry stuff. Not so the hymn, and it is time we turned to it and looked at some of the stanzas.

In the original version Bridges headed the hymn with the text, 'On his head were many crowns' (Rev. 19:12). It was the thought of the Redeemer's *many* crowns that arrested his attention, and his purpose was (somewhat fancifully) to attach a particular meaning to some of them.

> Crown him with many crowns,
> The Lamb upon his throne,
> Hark how the heavenly anthem drowns
> All music but its own.
> Awake, my soul, and sing
> Of him who died for thee,
> And hail him as thy matchless King
> Through all eternity.

Bridges' opening verse, common to all versions, makes an excellent introduction to the hymn. We are called upon to crown Jesus as 'the Lamb upon the throne' – pictorial language derived from the Revelation. The *Lamb* is the symbol of sacrifice, the *throne* the symbol of sovereignty. The two belong together. Christ is 'highly exalted' and reigns in glory because of his having been 'obedient unto death' (Phil. 2:8,9). The 'heavenly music' is that of the angels. 'Awake *my* soul and sing' is a gracious touch, inviting us to add our voices to theirs in singing the Redeemer's praise.

Bridges' second stanza is a celebration of the Incarnation and begins:

> Crown him the Virgin's Son,
> The God incarnate born.

The theme is excellent and the stanza starts well; but much of the later language is difficult. Not surprisingly Thring was unhappy with this and substituted a stanza of his own beginning:

> Crown him the Son of God
> Before the worlds began.

Several hymnals make use of this, but personally I do not think it is really up to standard. I much prefer the modified version of Bridges in the *BBC Hymn Book*, 1951, where the second half reads:

> The Saviour long foretold,
> The Branch of Jesse's stem,
> The eternal Shepherd of his fold,
> The Babe of Bethlehem.

★   ★   ★

From the Incarnation the hymn moves immediately to the Cross. Here is Bridges' third stanza:

> Crown him the Lord of love;
> Behold his hands and side,
> Those wounds yet visible above,
> In beauty glorified;
> No angel in the sky
> Can fully bear that sight,
> But downwards bends his burning eye
> At mysteries so bright.

This crown belongs to Jesus as the Lord of love. The cross is the supreme manifestation of his love for us sinners. As by faith we behold his pierced hands and side we are reminded that those sacred wounds are 'yet visible above', for Jesus ascended to the Father in his glorified resurrection body, still bearing the marks of his passion. In a vision St John saw the Lamb 'as though it had been slain' (Rev. 5:6). And as the angels adore the Lamb the hymn pictures them veiling their faces in the presence of so glorious a mystery.

From the cross to the empty tomb. Somewhat strangely

Bridges has no stanza on the Resurrection, but Thring admirably supplies this lack.

> Crown him the Lord of life,
>   Who triumphed o'er the grave,
> And rose victorious in the strife
>   For those he came to save.
>   His glories now we sing
>   Who died and rose on high,
> Who died eternal life to bring,
>   And lives that death may die.

The stanza calls for no particular comment, except to say that no version of the hymn should be without it. And while the words speak for themselves they are well worth reflecting on.

★   ★   ★

Back to Bridges, to whom of course chief credit must be given for this hymn. His stanza beginning 'Crown him the Lord of peace, whose power a sceptre sways' has a markedly contemporary ring about it. We live in a broken and warring world where everyone is longing for peace, talking about it, working towards it – but failing to find it. Surely it is well to be reminded that Jesus is the ultimate answer to the world's tragic need and that only in acknowledging his claims and submitting to his rule is peace a possibility between man and man, nation and nation.

The final stanza makes a majestic finish to the hymn. Here the praise we offer to our Lord is both cosmic (for he is the creator of the world) and personal (for he is the Redeemer who died for each one of us).

> Crown him the Lord of years,
>   The Potentate of time,
> Creator of the rolling spheres,
>   Ineffably sublime:

All hail, Redeemer, hail!
For thou hast died for me;
Thy praise shall never, never fail
Throughout eternity.

10

FOR THE BEAUTY OF THE EARTH
F.S. Pierpoint, 1835–1917

This popular hymn of praise is found in hymnals in virtually two different forms. In its original form it is, as its author intended, specifically a communion hymn and has eight stanzas. In the other form, as it appears in most books, it is cut down to five stanzas and is a general hymn of praise. We are adopting this second version as being both the shorter and the more widely known.

*　　*　　*

There is not a lot to be said about the author. Folliott Sandford Pierpoint was a West Countryman, born in Bath and educated at the local grammar school. He later graduated as a classical scholar at Cambridge, took holy orders and became a devout Anglican priest in the Catholic tradition. In the course of a long life he wrote a good deal of verse, including a number of hymns. It is by this one alone, published in 1864, that he is now remembered. It can be found in its complete form in the *English Hymnal*.

> For the beauty of the earth,
>   For the beauty of the skies,
> For the love which from our birth
>   Over and around us lies:
>   *Christ our God, to thee we raise*
>   *This our sacrifice of praise.*

The refrain, sung after each stanza, is printed here as Pierpoint wrote it, the 'sacrifice of praise' being the eucharistic sacrifice. It is given in amended forms in some books.

It is said that the hymn was suggested to its author by the view from a hilltop outside Bath in the spring. The beauty of the landscape caused him to reflect on the gifts of God in creation and this is the theme of the opening stanzas.

The first declares that the beauty of the earth and sky is not only a revelation of God's creative power. It is also a token of his love, the love that encircles our lives from our birth till the end of our days. God has placed us in a world full of lovely things; but while we praise him for that, we praise him most for his loving kindness and concern for the happiness of his children.

But more:

> For the beauty of each hour
>   Of the day and of the night,
> Hill and vale, and tree and flower,
>   Sun and moon and stars of light.

There *is* beauty in each hour, if we have eyes to see it. And certainly the night has its beauty as well as the day, the sky as well as the earth. We look *around* in God's world and survey the glory of 'hill and vale, and tree and flower' with their infinite variety of size and form and colour. We look *up* and see his handiwork no less in 'sun and moon and stars of light'. As the psalmist declares, 'The heavens tell out the glory of God', and their vastness not only enlarges our vision of the Creator, but fills our hearts with wonder and praise.

★　　★　　★

In the next stanza we praise God for our physical faculties.

> For the joy of ear and eye,
>   For the heart and brain's delight,
> For the mystic harmony
>   Linking sense to sound and sight.

How fitting it is that we should praise God for hearing and sight. So much of our enjoyment of life is dependent on them. Yet too readily we take these faculties for granted and seldom think of what it would be like to live in a world of silence or darkness.

And there is the spiritual aspect of the matter, referred to in the second half of the verse. We have power to appreciate inwardly (with 'heart and brain') what we see and hear with our eyes and ears. This is what the hymn calls 'the mystic harmony' which links *sense* (feeling, understanding) to what we hear and see. The link is between the spiritual and the physical, the inward and the outward.

Another subject for praise lies in the realm of family and friends.

> For the joy of human love,
>   Brother, sister, parent, child,
> Friends on earth, and friends above,
>   For all gentle thoughts and mild.

Here everything is straightforward and seems to require little comment. But the words must not be hurriedly passed over without due reflection. What would our lives be without 'the joy of human love'? The bonds of family life, 'brother, sister, parent, child', are precious indeed, worth more than riches or fame. The same is true of the gift of friendship, which has a wider scope than the family and sometimes must take the place of it. This circle includes not only friends on earth but those in heaven who have gone before us in the way of faith.

★   ★   ★

> For each perfect gift of thine
>   To our race so freely given,
> Graces human and divine,
>   Flowers of earth and buds of heaven.

In the hymn's final verse in its present form our praise is on a universal scale. We rejoice in every good and perfect gift which the Father has so freely bestowed on us, and not only on us but on the whole race. All that is clear enough. But what are we to make of the final line, 'Flowers of earth and buds of heaven'?

To understand it we must link the line closely with the preceding one, 'Graces human and divine'. The two lines belong together and form a couplet.

The 'flowers of earth' are the 'human graces', the natural endowments which are developed now and adorn our present life. The 'buds of heaven' are the divine graces which are only partially realised on earth and await their fulfilment in the life to come.

Think about it. But however we interpret the words the response of our hearts is the same:

> *Christ our God, to thee we raise*
> *This our sacrifice of praise.*

11

HOW SHALL I SING THAT MAJESTY
John Mason, 1645–94

This hymn may not be as familiar to some readers as most of the others in this book. This is not altogether surprising, for though it was written 300 years ago it has not been in general use until fairly recently.

John Mason, the man who wrote it, was an interesting and to some extent an important character. His father, a humble Dissenting minister, struggled hard to give his son the best possible education. Thus it came about that he graduated at Cambridge, was ordained, and eventually in 1673 was appointed rector of Water-Stratford, Bucks, where he spent the rest of his life.

It was there that he published his collection of hymns, *Songs of Praise*, 1683, this one among them. It seems clear that he intended the hymns to be sung in public worship, although at that time hymn-singing was virtually unknown in the Church of England. Nevertheless, the book went through twenty editions, and John Mason must be credited as one of the pioneers of the English hymn.

His life was comparatively uneventful until his last month, when he created a sensation by announcing that he had seen a vision of Jesus crowned with glory which predicted the imminence of his second coming – which would take place at Water-Stratford! Crowds flocked to the parish from far and wide in expectation of the Advent. Extraordinary scenes occurred with frenzied singing and dancing. The excitement had scarcely abated when Mason was taken ill and died – a sad end for a man

who had been a faithful and high-esteemed minister of
Christ.

⋆   ⋆   ⋆

Mason's hymns were immensely popular for a time, but
within a generation or two they were almost completely
supplanted by the hymns of Watts and Wesley. Our hymn,
'How shall I sing that Majesty', was virtually lost to sight
for two centuries until it appeared in the *English Hymnal*,
1906.

It is a hymn about worship, and more especially about the
God to whom we in our sinful state presume to offer our
praise.

> How shall I sing that Majesty
>   Which angels do admire?
> Let dust in dust and silence lie;
>   Sing, sing, ye heavenly choir.
> Thousands and thousands stand around
>   Thy throne, O God most high;
> Ten thousand times ten thousand sound
>   Thy praise; but who am I?

The writer is impressed, almost oppressed, by the majesty
of God: his royalty, his transcendence, his splendour. He
felt something like Faber when he wrote 'My God, how
wonderful thou art' (Chapter 16). If we, too, felt like that,
if we had a bigger idea of God and a smaller idea of
ourselves, our worship would doubtless be of a more
exalted character, and we should be lost in wonder, love and
praise.

As it is, most of us are too high-minded, too earthbound,
to give serious consideration to the question with which
John Mason begins his hymn. In its entirety it teaches us to
be more humble in our worship: to bow our hearts as well as
our heads in the presence of the almighty King. Only so
shall we sing words like these with a sense of spiritual
reality. When we consider that 'ten thousand times ten

thousand' angels surround God's throne and ceaselessly chant his praise, well may we ask, 'But who am I?' The second stanza follows up this question.

*   *   *

Thy brightness unto them appears,
    Whilst I thy footsteps trace;
A sound of God comes to my ears,
    But they behold thy face;
They sing because thou art their sun:
    Lord, send a beam on me;
For where heaven is but once begun
    There Alleluias be.

The stanza draws a series of contrasts between the angels' worship and our own. *They* enjoy far higher privileges than do we. To them the Lord directly reveals his 'brightness', the brightness of his presence amid the splendour of heaven. But we know nothing of that. It lies outside our present experience. We can but trace his 'footsteps', his ways with men, as they are revealed to us in his Word.

A 'sound of God' thus comes to our ears, that sound being the voice of divine revelation. But that is as far as we can go at present. The beatific vision of the angels is not ours as yet: 'they behold thy face'. For now we must be content to see in a mirror dimly; but at last, like the angels, we shall see God face to face (1 Cor. 13:12).

The last part of the stanza is a prayer. The angels sing because God is their 'sun'. We ask, 'Lord, send a beam on me', so that heaven may already begin for us and we may add our Alleluias to their praise.

*   *   *

The final stanza returns to the theme of God's majesty.

How great a being, Lord, is thine,
    Which doth all beings keep!

> Thy knowledge is the only line
>   To sound so vast a deep.
> Thou art a sea without a shore,
>   A sun without a sphere;
> Thy time is now and evermore,
>   Thy place is everywhere.

What a lot of things this tells us about God! Note them in turn.

First, the greatness of his being as the one who has all beings, including all humanity, in his keeping.

Next, the depth of his knowledge, his omniscience, so vast a depth that no line could ever fathom it.

Third, his infinity, boundless as 'a sea without a shore, a sun without a sphere'.

Fourth, his eternity: his 'time is now and evermore', for with him time has no existence.

Finally, his omnipresence: 'thy place is everywhere'.

Certainly here are words to think about as well as to sing. To sing them without thought would be of little help. Yet their appeal is to the heart as well as to the head, so as to give us a wider and grander view of the God who, like the angels, we worship and adore.

12

IMMORTAL, INVISIBLE, GOD ONLY WISE
W. Chalmers Smith, 1824–1908

While this hymn of praise is a favourite, it is not altogether an easy one. Worshippers are inclined to sing it with great gusto, carried along by the lilting Welsh tune *St Denio*; but how much do the *words* actually mean to them?

Perhaps I am doing them an injustice, but undeniably the hymn has certain difficulties, even obscurities. The American hymnologist Albert Bailey described it as a 'rather florid attempt to express the inexpressible' and said it does more to stimulate the imagination than to clarify thought. Let us see what we can make of its rhetorical language and its variety of metaphors.

★   ★   ★

The hymn is essentially a celebration of God as the Creator of the universe, inspired by the words of 1 Timothy 1:17 (AV): 'Now unto the King eternal, immortal, invisible, the only wise God, be honour and glory for ever and ever.' Thus it begins:

> Immortal, invisible, God only wise,
> In light inaccessible hid from our eyes,
> Most blessed, most glorious, the Ancient of Days,
> Almighty, victorious, thy great name we praise.

Note particularly the second line: 'In light inaccessible hid from our eyes'. *Light* is the basic metaphor of the hymn. It occurs in three of the four stanzas. The word is used frequently in Scripture to describe God. St John wrote, 'God is light, and in him is no darkness at all' (1 John 1:5). Or in the words of Psalm 104:2, 'who coverest thyself with light as with a garment' (AV). Yet, says the hymn, the light of God is 'inaccessible', hidden from our eyes. The explanation seems to be that while light reveals it also dazzles and obscures its source. The best illustration of this is the light of the sun. In this sense God is invisible and beyond our sight.

The stanza as a whole is occupied with the glory of God, the God whose great name we praise: 'Most blessed, most glorious, the Ancient of Days, almighty, victorious'. 'The Ancient of Days' is an Old Testament expression denoting that God is eternal. Such, then, is the majestic picture of God that confronts us at the outset and it makes an excellent beginning to the hymn.

The next stanza tells us more of what God is like.

Unresting, unhasting, and silent as light,
Nor wanting, nor wasting, thou rulest in might;
Thy justice like mountains high soaring above,
Thy clouds which are fountains of goodness and love.

In the words 'thou rulest in might' there is a recognition of the sovereignty of God and the hymn never gets far from that. But the stanza as a whole is about the *immutability* of God. He is unchanging and unchangeable. This is the underlying meaning of the phrases 'unresting, unhasting' and 'nor wanting, nor wasting'. Note the further reference to *light* in the striking words 'silent as light', descriptive of how God rules and works.

In the last two lines we have the metaphors of the mountains and the clouds. The towering mountains, solid and immovable, are symbolic of God's absolute justice in his dealings with his world and with his creatures.

What of the clouds? As they continually water the earth and so sustain the life of mankind they resemble God's goodness and mercy which follow us all our days. They remind us of the 'showers of blessing' with which he visits his people. The just God is also and always the God of love.

★   ★   ★

> To all life thou givest, to both great and small;
> In all life thou livest, the true life of all;
> We blossom and flourish as leaves on the tree,
> And wither and perish – but nought changeth thee.

Life is the repeated and emphatic word in this stanza. God is the source of life, the giver of life, the sustainer of life. All things living owe their life to him. Man cannot manufacture life. It is the gift of the Creator.

'In all life thou livest, the true life of all.' This line has been questioned as having a 'pantheistic' ring about it. Pantheism (from the Greek *pan* 'all', and *theos* 'God') is the ancient belief or philosophy that God has no independent existence. God is everything and everything is God. In other words, the Creator and creation are one.

Such nonsense is quite inconsistent with Christianity and the hymn has nothing to do with it. What the writer is saying is that everything has God as its innermost reality. And that is true of humanity as well: 'in him we live, and move, and have our being' (Acts 17:28 AV).

The last two lines employ another metaphor drawn from the natural world, that of the leaves of a tree which flourish for a time and later 'wither and perish'. This illustrates the changeable character of man's brief life on earth. But God is not like that: 'nought changeth thee.'

> Great Father of glory, pure Father of light,
> Thine angels adore thee, all veiling their sight;
> All laud we would render: O help us to see
> 'Tis only the splendour of light hideth thee.

The hymn begins with praise and ends with praise. Once again we are reminded of the infinite greatness of God as the

'Father of glory' and 'Father of light', adored by the angels in heaven. But they are not alone in their worship. 'All laud *we* would render', and as we do so we recognise that since God dwells in 'unapproachable light' and that no man has ever seen him or can see him (1 Tim. 6:16) it is not the lack of light but the excess of it that hides him from us.

★   ★   ★

So far we have said nothing about the distinguished Scottish minister who wrote this hymn. Dr Walter Chalmers Smith was born in Aberdeen and educated at the city's grammar school and university. He won recognition in the Free Church of Scotland as preacher and scholar, and finally as Moderator.

He said that he wrote his hymns as 'a retreat from the burdens of his labours'. But it seems that they lacked the common touch, for of the many he wrote none has survived except 'Immortal, invisible'. This is a fine hymn indeed when rightly understood; but just possibly it owes its survival to its tune as much as to its words.

13

LET ALL THE WORLD IN EVERY CORNER SING
George Herbert, 1593–1632

This is one of the shortest hymns of praise in our hymn-books; but for all its brevity, what a gem it is! We soon learn not to judge the worth of a hymn by its length. A long hymn may easily become boring. A short one never has that effect. I guarantee that no one has ever been bored by singing this hymn to the fine tune *Luckington*, which Basil Harwood composed for it in 1908.

★   ★   ★

George Herbert was one of the foremost poets of the seventeenth century. He belonged to an old and distinguished English family, the Herberts being of Norman descent. He was born at Montgomery Castle, the ancestral seat on the Welsh borders, and educated at Westminster School and Cambridge. At the university he proved himself to be a fine scholar, and after winning various academic honours he was appointed University Orator.

At the age of 23 he seemed to be on the brink of a brilliant career. Favoured by James I and other influential people he had entered the life of the Court; but his hopes of preferment were dashed by the death of the king.

He had come to a turning-point in his life. For some months he retired from London society and lived in seclusion with a friend in Kent. Here he passed through a spiritual crisis. He had been an ambitious and proud man, seeking great things for himself. Now his life took on a new direction. He turned his back on the world and, as he wrote later, he subjected his soul to the will of Jesus his Master.

The immediate outcome was that he decided to take holy orders. Soon afterwards he married and spent the last four years of his life as vicar of Bemerton, a small village near Salisbury. Here he proved himself a model pastor and priest. Here also he wrote most of his religious verse. His health rapidly declined and he died at the age of 40. Shortly afterwards his poetical works were published in a book called *The Temple*, and it is from this that his 'hymns', as we know them, are derived.

★   ★   ★

In *The Temple* the poem 'Let all the world in every corner sing' is headed 'Antiphon'. This provides the key to its structure. The word antiphon comes from the Greek (*anti*, 'in return', and *phone*, 'voice'), so that it describes a form of church music sung by two groups, each responding to the other.

Before proceeding further let us note that in entitling his poem as he did, George Herbert obviously intended it to be *sung*. But where? And by whom? Not in church or by the congregation, for in his time the singing of hymns was not part of public worship in the Church of England. The singing was restricted to the metrical psalms, the biblical psalms put into metre and rhyme.

Clearly then he did not write his religious songs to be sung in church. His intention was that they should be sung in the home, in the family circle, to the accompaniment of lute or viol. Herbert himself was a gifted musician and wrote many tunes for his poems.

In his manuscript he indicated how his antiphon was to be sung by the two groups. There was the *chorus* (the first two lines) which was repeated and in which everyone was to join; and there were the *verses* (the four lines that follow) to be sung by a smaller number, such as a choir or quartet.

The hymn is seldom if ever sung in this form, but it could easily be done and would be what the poet intended.

★   ★   ★

So now to the words, and first to the chorus:

> Let all the world in every corner sing,
>   My God and King.

The words are repeated at the beginning and end of each stanza. We notice at once the breadth of the appeal or invitation. It is addressed to 'all the world' and to every corner of the world. It is a universal call to praise. One can but reflect that if only the world at large were to heed that call, what a different world it would be.

But there is the personal side as well: '*My* God and King.' This is where we come in. *My God* – who is he? My God is the one I worship, the one who has first place in my life, the one I love with all my heart and soul and strength.

And then *my King*. Who is he? My King is the one to whom I owe my primary loyalty and allegiance, the one I am pledged to serve and obey. God is both my God and my King (Ps. 68:24). The titles are complementary.

★   ★   ★

Finally there are the two verses. Both consist of a contrasting pair of couplets. Thus the first:

> The heavens are not too high,
> His praise may thither fly;
> The earth is not too low,
> His praises there may grow.

The contrast here is between the heavens and the earth. However high the heavens may be – probably not in the literal but in the spiritual sense – 'his praise may thither fly' and reach the abode of God in his infinite glory. By contrast, the earth which is *our* abode is not too mean or poor a place for his praises to be heard – and not only heard but to 'grow', everywhere increasing and abounding.

So to the second verse:

> The Church with psalms must shout,
> No door can keep them out;
> But above all the heart
> Must bear the longest part.

The contrast now is between the public worship of the Church, with its psalms and other praises, and the private devotion of the heart. This latter is 'above all', that is, of the greater importance, for it 'must bear the longest part'. The longest, note, not the loudest! The poet here reminds us that while the Church's official acts of worship take place only at certain times and on certain days, the praise of the heart is unceasing: it is prolonged through every hour and every day of life.

14

'LIFT UP YOUR HEARTS!' WE LIFT THEM, LORD, TO THEE
H. Montagu Butler, 1833–1918

This hymn was first sung in the chapel of the famous Harrow School, and that was more than a century ago. With a little imagination you can picture the scene. The splendid school chapel is packed with hundreds of boys singing the challenging words with lusty voices, and with some pride, knowing that the hymn has been written expressly for them by their headmaster.

That headmaster was Henry Montagu Butler, one of the most brilliant scholars of his day. His name is inevitably associated with Harrow, for his father had been headmaster before him and he himself had been educated there. And when at the early age of 26 he was appointed to the headship he revolutionised the life of the school. In the past it had adhered rigidly to the old classical tradition. He introduced the study of science and modernised the whole approach to education.

By all accounts Dr Butler was an outstanding man. He has been described as a great inspirer whose life radiated a spiritual energy which deeply influenced the boys and to which they reacted accordingly. Among those thus influenced were many of the future leaders of the nation. He left Harrow in 1885 to become Dean of Gloucester and was later Vice-Chancellor of Cambridge University.

★　　★　　★

The hymn by which his memory lives on was written for the *Harrow School Hymn-Book*, 1881. It draws its inspiration from the *Sursum corda* in the communion service: 'Lift up your hearts!', to which the congregation makes its response, 'We lift them up to the Lord'. The words are of very early origin and are first quoted by St Cyprian, the third-century Bishop of Carthage.

> 'Lift up your hearts!' We lift them, Lord, to thee;
> Here at thy feet none other may we see:
> 'Lift up your hearts!' E'en so, with one accord,
> We lift them up, we lift them to the Lord.

Cyprian taught that the design of the *Sursum corda* was to summon the worshippers at the Eucharist to concentrate their minds wholly and purposefully on the Lord. It is a needful piece of spiritual counsel for Christian congregations of all times. As we know well enough, in our worship our thoughts all too readily stray. Instead of dwelling on God they become occupied with other things, lesser things, our own petty concerns.

Perhaps to some extent this is inevitable, and no doubt the Lord understands. But at this point in the service, leading into the great Thanksgiving, or eucharistic prayer, it is right that we should be called to lift up our hearts from the things of earth to the things of heaven, from the transient to the eternal, from ourselves to God.

Dr Butler conveys this thought in the line 'Here at thy feet none other may we see'; and in the last line he is emphatic: 'We lift them up, we lift them to the *Lord*.'

                    ★   ★   ★

The subsequent stanzas become more specific and personal.

> Above the level of the former years,
> The mire of sin, the slough of guilty fears,
> The mist of doubt, the blight of love's decay,
> O Lord of Light, lift all our hearts today!

Our lives in general are too earthbound. In the past ('the former years') our spiritual level has been too low. The call that comes to us is to lift both our hearts and our lives to a higher plane.

Dr Butler has his schoolboys much in mind in the expressions and metaphors he employs. He wants to remind them that sin is a dirty thing which besmirches character; that a bad conscience ('guilty fears') gets us bogged down and hinders spiritual progress; that doubt obscures our vision of God; and that love, the highest and purest of all virtues, can degenerate and decay.

These are things that belong to the dark and shady side of life. Our prayer is that the Lord will lift us above them into the realm of light, his own light of holiness and love.

The next stanza is equally outspoken.

> Above the swamps of subterfuge and shame,
> The deeds, the thoughts, that honour may not name,
> The halting tongue that dares not tell the whole,
> O Lord of Truth, lift every Christian soul!

If we know anything about ourselves we shall have no difficulty in recognising the reality of the sins mentioned here: cowardice, dishonour, hypocrisy, falsehood. Well may we pray the 'Lord of Truth' to lift us far above such things, for they are all enemies of the truth and of our souls' highest good.

★   ★   ★

But there is something more we must face as we lift up our hearts to God.

> Lift every gift that thou thyself hast given;
> Low lies the best till lifted up to heaven:
> Low lie the bounding heart, the teeming brain,
> Till, sent from God, they mount to God again.

In these arresting words we are bidden to lift to God *every* good gift he has bestowed on us, for 'low lies the best till lifted up to heaven'. Our gifts and talents vary enormously, but they all come from God, and not only are we responsible to him for how we use them; they must be offered back to him who gave them. Man's most brilliant gifts never achieve their true worth until lifted up to God and dedicated to his service. Indeed, such gifts unless so dedicated may achieve evil rather than good in the world.

The hymn ends with a final reminder that it was originally written with schoolboys in mind.

> Then, as the trumpet-call, in after years,
> 'Lift up your hearts!' rings pealing in our ears,
> Still shall those hearts respond with full accord,
> 'We lift them up, we lift them to the Lord!'

The second stanza spoke of 'the former years' and alluded to the past. Here the reference is to life's 'after years', the unknown future which stretched before the young Harrovians and which for them was all-important.

All through their lives the trumpet-call 'Lift up your hearts' would continue to sound in their ears with undiminished urgency. Their religion was not to end when they left school. And that call was not only to be heard. It was also to be heeded and to win from their hearts the same response: 'We lift them up, we lift them to the Lord!'

15

LORD, ENTHRONED IN HEAVENLY SPLENDOUR
G.H. Bourne, 1840–1925

Like 'Alleluia! sing to Jesus' (Chapter 3) this was written as a communion hymn for Ascensiontide. Like the other, too, it is sometimes sung on other occasions, but is essentially a hymn for the Eucharist.

It has the advantage of a splendid tune, *St Helen*, which Sir George Martin composed for it when it first appeared in *Hymns Ancient and Modern*, 1889. But that apart, it is assuredly a good hymn, and a good hymn deserves a good tune.

★   ★   ★

The author of the hymn, George Hugh Bourne, was educated at Eton and graduated at Oxford with the degree of DCL. After ordination he spent a large part of his life in educational work and from 1874 to 1885 he was headmaster of St Edmund's School, Salisbury.

It was during those years that he published, privately, his *Seven Post-Communion Hymns* for use in the school. This one originally consisted of ten stanzas – far too long for normal use, and hard luck on the boys! Our hymn-books today considerably reduce its length. We shall reflect on the five stanzas most commonly used.

> Lord, enthroned in heavenly splendour,
>   First-begotten from the dead,
> Thou alone, our strong Defender,

Liftest up thy people's head.
Alleluia!
Jesu, true and living Bread.

We are reminded at the outset that this is an Ascensiontide hymn. It is addressed to the exalted Lord, enthroned in glory at the right hand of the Father. The portrait is enlarged in the series of descriptive phrases that follow.

Christ is the 'First-begotten from the dead' – a New Testament expression (Col. 1:18) which refers to his resurrection and is linked with his pre-eminence in all things. By his resurrection he won the final victory over death, that others might rise with him and partake of his victory.

Again, the risen and reigning Christ is his people's 'strong defender' who 'lifts up their heads' – a Bible expression which means that he exalts them on high, so that they may share his heavenly glory.

For this we sing 'Alleluia' and praise him who is the 'true and living Bread'. More is said about that in the final stanza.

Here our humblest homage pay we;
Here in loving reverence bow;
Here for faith's discernment pray thee,
Lest we fail to know thee now.
Alleluia!
Thou art here, we ask not how.

We approach the sacrament in a deeply humble spirit, bowing before the Lord 'in loving reverence' and yielding him due homage as our King. In no part of our Christian worship is such humility and reverence more necessary than when we come to the Lord's table.

And therefore we come with a prayer in our hearts, a prayer for 'faith's discernment' – that is for spiritual perception of the Lord's person and presence in the sacrament. St Paul utters a warning about 'not discerning the body' when we partake of the bread and wine (1 Cor. 11:29). The hymn refers to this in the line 'Lest we fail to know thee now'. The

Lord's presence is real ('thou art here') and it is important
that we should recognise the fact, however little we may be
able to explain 'how'. The next stanza says something more
about it.

> Though the lowliest form doth veil thee
>   As of old in Bethlehem,
> Here as there thine angels hail thee,
>   Branch and Flower of Jesse's stem.
>   Alleluia!
>   We in worship join with them.

The Lord's presence was veiled in lowliest form in the
mystery of the Incarnation. As Charles Wesley wrote,
'Veiled in flesh the Godhead see!' So in the sacrament of the
Lord's supper his presence is now veiled under the outward
forms of bread and wine.

'Here as there thine angels hail thee.' The angels certainly
hailed the Lord's birth at Bethlehem and it may not be
unduly fanciful to imagine that they surround us now as in
worship we join with them.

The words 'Branch and Flower of Jesse's stem' allude to
Jesus as the Son of David, based on Isaiah 11:1.

★   ★   ★

The last two stanzas also have an Old Testament background, derived from the Book of Exodus.

> Pascal Lamb, thine offering, finished
>   Once for all when thou wast slain,
> In its fullness undiminished
>   Shall for evermore remain,
>   Alleluia!
>   Cleansing souls from every stain.

The title 'Pascal Lamb' takes us back to the Passover (Exod.
12) when in each household a lamb was slain and its blood

sprinkled to secure the emancipation of the enslaved
Israelites from Egypt. This is used in the New Testament as
an illustration of Christ's saving and liberating work on the
cross. Thus St Paul: 'Christ, our pascal lamb, has been
sacrificed' (1 Cor. 5:7 RSV).

In the sacrament we commemorate his sacrifice. We call it
vividly to mind. We set it forth in visible form. We make
ourselves one with it. We claim its benefits for ourselves.
The thing we cannot do is to *repeat* it. His offering was
'finished once for all' and 'in its fullness' remains for ever
our only salvation.

> Life-imparting heavenly Manna,
>   Stricken Rock with streaming side,
> Heaven and earth with loud hosannas
>   Worship thee, the Lamb who died.
>   Alleluia!
>   Risen, ascended, glorified!

This final stanza draws on two other Exodus stories to
illustrate what Christ is to his people. He is the 'heavenly
Manna', the true bread from heaven who gives life to the
world (John 6:33). He is also the 'stricken Rock' from
which water streamed in the desert for the dying Israelites
(Exod. 17): a picture of the crucified Saviour from whom
flows 'living water', that those who drink may thirst no
more (John 4:10–14).

All these Biblical allusions point to Christ, and therefore
the hymn ends on a splendid note of adoration in which
heaven and earth unite to praise the exalted Lord – 'Risen,
ascended, glorified!'

16

MY GOD, HOW WONDERFUL THOU ART
F. W. Faber, 1814–63

You may question whether this is really a hymn of praise, but it is certainly a magnificent act of worship. And praise and worship are intimately linked together. Praise is the principal part of worship, though of course worship includes other elements, several of which have a place in this hymn.

It is a hymn well worth looking at, for it has a teaching content as well as spiritual depth.

★　　★　　★

Frederick William Faber's parents were strict Calvinists, but early in life he joined the Church of England and moved towards the Catholic wing. Educated at Harrow and Balliol College, Oxford, he was ordained in 1837; but shortly afterwards he came under the influence of Newman and the Tractarian Movement. The outcome was that in 1845 he was received into the Roman Catholic Church and re-ordained.

Faber never forgot how in his early life the evangelical hymns of Wesley, Newton and Cowper had 'acted like a spell' upon him, and now he felt the need of some popular hymns of a similar character for Roman Catholics. Having a genuine poetic gift he set himself the task of writing the sort of hymns required. In the course of his ministry he wrote 150, the number of the Psalms. Among those still being sung are 'Souls of men, why will ye scatter' and 'Sweet

Saviour, bless us ere we go', in addition to 'My God, how wonderful thou art'.

This latter is undoubtedly Faber's finest hymn. He headed it 'The Eternal Father', so it is a hymn about God. It could have no nobler theme. It tells us who God is, what he is like, and how we are to worship him.

> My God, how wonderful thou art,
>   Thy majesty how bright,
> How beautiful thy mercy-seat,
>   In depths of burning light.

The hymn opens on a note of wonder. Wonder at what? Is there anything left for us to wonder at in today's world? The answer is, Yes – God himself. He is the supreme wonder.

In his study of this hymn Dr Erik Routley says that the great question it puts to the Christian is, 'When did you last consciously and purposely practise the sacred employment of wonder?' And the answer to that, surely, is another question: 'When did you last deliberately contemplate God in his eternal glory?'

So often our God is too small. This hymn helps us to take a bigger view of him and here in the first stanza we catch a glimpse of the brightness of his majesty, the beauty of his mercy, the blazing splendour of his light.

★   ★   ★

In the same spirit of wonder and worship the hymn continues:

> How dread are thine eternal years,
>   O everlasting Lord,
> By prostrate spirits day and night
>   Incessantly adored!

God is eternal. He has neither beginning nor end. To speak of his 'eternal years' is an intentional anomaly. Years belong

to the world of time, our world. God exists entirely outside
that world and inhabits eternity. He is the 'everlasting Lord'
and as such he is endlessly extolled and adored by the spirits
of men and angels.

> How wonderful, how beautiful,
>   The sight of thee must be,
> Thine endless wisdom, boundless power,
>   And aweful purity!

'How wonderful' – yes again. In our progress through this
hymn we are still in wonderland. But it is not a dream-
world as it was in the case of Alice. It is utterly real, as real as
God himself.

How wonderful – yes, and 'how beautiful'! Beauty is not
something we often attribute to God, but it is part of his
moral perfection. The psalmist was aware of this when he
prayed, 'Let the beauty of the Lord our God be upon us' (Ps.
90:17).

The verse ends by exemplifying other of his attributes:
'Thine endless wisdom, boundless power, and aweful
purity.' These are words which call for little comment
but a lot of thought. They show us something more of
what God is like: all wise, all powerful, all holy.

★   ★   ★

If such be our vision of God, what should be our reaction or
response?

> O how I fear thee, living God,
>   With deepest, tenderest fears,
> And worship thee with trembling hope,
>   And penitential tears!

The first and most logical reaction is to *fear* God. The Bible
has a lot to say about that. 'The fear of the Lord is the
beginning of wisdom' (Ps. 111:10). But what does it mean

to fear God? It certainly does not mean to be afraid of him. To fear God is to reverence him, to recognise his holiness, majesty and power, and to obey his will.

Faber says that he will fear God, 'the living God', and *worship* him. That is the heart of the matter. The fear of God is expressed most naturally in the worship of God: worship that is offered not with arrogance but with 'trembling hope', not with pride but with 'penitential tears'.

But fear is not our only reaction to the sight of God.

> Yet I may love thee too, O Lord,
>   Almighty as thou art,
> For thou hast stooped to ask of me
>   The love of my poor heart.

So a corresponding question arises. What does it mean to *love* God? For one thing, quite obviously, it means to know God, for you cannot consciously love someone you do not know. To know God is not simply to know about him in text-book fashion, but to know him personally as your loving Father.

Love is also closely related to devotion. To love God is to be devoted to him: not sentimentally but with a true deep loyalty and dedication. And of course another element in love is gratitude. You love those most who have done most for you. So with our love for God. We love because he first loved us and in Christ wrought our eternal salvation.

     ★   ★   ★

The theme of God's love is continued:

> No earthly father loves like thee,
>   No mother half so mild
> Bears and forbears, as thou hast done
>   With me, thy sinful child.

These tender words remind us that God's love does not belong only to the past when he gave his Son to die for us. It is a present and continuing reality. He loves us now and for ever. That being so, what better can we do than pray:

> Oh, then, this worse than worthless heart
>   In pity deign to take,
> And make it love thee for thyself
>   And for thy glory's sake.

17

NOW THANK WE ALL OUR GOD
Martin Rinkart, 1586–1649,
trs. Catherine Winkworth, 1827–78

Those who comment on this celebrated German hymn of
thanksgiving are accustomed to point out that it was
written during the horrific days of the Thirty Years War. Its
author, Martin Rinkart, was the Lutheran pastor of his
native town of Eilenberg, Saxony, which became a refuge
for homeless people from far and wide. Pestilence and
famine followed in the train of war. Terrible conditions
prevailed and the death-rate was appalling. When things
were at their worst Rinkart sometimes conducted up to fifty
funerals a day. Such a state of affairs was hardly conducive
to composing a hymn of thanksgiving.

But in fact the lines were not originally written as a
hymn. Rinkart wrote them – the first two stanzas only – as a
grace to be sung at meals in his own household. They were
designed simply for domestic use. The third stanza, a
Trinitarian doxology, was not added till some time later, to
make a hymn suitable for Christian worship.

In this form it was translated, more than 200 years later,
by Miss Catherine Winkworth, who specialised in this
work. For another example, see Chapter 23.

★   ★   ★

The first two stanzas are a free paraphrase of Ecclesiasticus
50:22–4 (RSV):

> Now bless the God of all,
>> Who in every way does great things;

Who exalts our days from birth,
   And deals with us according to his mercy.
May he give us gladness of heart,
   And grant that peace may be in our days in Israel,
   As in the days of old.
May he entrust to us his mercy,
   And let him deliver us in our days!

These words combine both thanksgiving and prayer, and this is true also of the hymn. The first stanza strikes the note of thanksgiving and looks back to the *past*. The second is an act of prayer and seeks God's grace and mercy for the *future*.

Now thank we all our God,
   With heart and hands and voices;
      Who wondrous things hath done,
   In whom his world rejoices.

These opening lines set the keynote of the hymn. We are *all* without exception to give thanks to God and we are told how we ought to do so: with *heart*, from the depths of our being; with *hands*, in our everyday deeds and activities; and with *voices*, in word and song, and especially in our worship.

The hymn goes on to speak of the wonderful works of God 'in whom his world rejoices'. God's world here is surely the world of nature, as in several of the Psalms. Creation rejoices in its Creator and in its own way gives him praise. For a further comment on this, see 'O praise ye the Lord!' (Chapter 20).

The remaining lines tell why we human beings are to thank our God:

Who from our mother's arms
   Hath blessed us on our way
With countless gifts of love,
   And still is ours today.

God 'exalts our days from birth', as the Ecclesiasticus passage puts it. Whatever our age, however long or short a time we have lived, we can gratefully acknowledge that 'from our mother's arms', from life's very beginning, God has blessed us 'with countless gifts of love'. Countless indeed! To attempt to *count* our blessings, as the chorus urges us to do, is really an impossible task. It is like trying to count the stars. But the greatest blessing of all is not what God gives us, but what he is to us. He 'still is ours *today*'. However we are placed, whatever we have or lack, nothing can rob us of God or separate us from his love (Rom. 8:38–9).

★   ★   ★

In the second stanza thanksgiving gives place to prayer, a prayer which echoes the petitions in Ecclesiasticus.

> O may this bounteous God
> Through all our life be near us,
>   With ever joyful hearts,
> And blessèd peace to cheer us;
>   And keep us in his grace,
>   And guide us when perplexed,
>   And free us from all ills,
>   In this world and the next.

The prayer begins by asking that our 'bounteous God', for whose goodness and generosity we have given thanks, may be with us 'through all our life', till its very end. If he is always near us and we have the assurance of that fact we can face whatever comes without fear or anxiety. For he will bless us with 'ever joyful hearts' and 'blessèd peace'. Here are two of God's richest gifts, worth more than anything the world can give or money can buy.

The second part of the stanza is a prayer that God will do three things for us. First, that he will 'keep us in his grace', for it is tragically possible to fall from grace and be ensnared by the world, the flesh and the devil.

Next we ask God to 'guide us when perplexed'; and who is not perplexed at times amid the many problems of life? To pray for God's guidance is as necessary as to pray for his grace.

The third petition is all-embracing: that God may 'free us from all ills, in this world and the next'. These last words remind us that we are citizens of two worlds. We need to keep *both* in mind as we journey through this present life to that which is to come.

★   ★   ★

The third stanza, as we have noted, was added later and takes the form of a Trinitarian doxology. Here we are singing 'Glory be to the Father, and to the Son, and to the Holy Spirit, now and for ever.'

> All praise and thanks to God
> The Father now be given,
>   The Son, and him who reigns
> With them in highest heaven;
>   The one eternal God,
>   Whom earth and heaven adore,
>   For thus it was, is now,
>   And shall be evermore.

'Him who reigns' with the Father and the Son is of course the Holy Spirit. This apart, the words of the stanza call for no particular comment. But how splendid and majestic is this final outburst of praise to the eternal Trinity! And how fittingly it rounds off this great hymn which, with its splendid tune by Rinkart's contemporary Johann Cruger (1598–1662), has been called the German *Te Deum*. But it is a universal hymn which transcends all national boundaries and is known and sung the whole world over.

18

O LORD OF HEAVEN AND EARTH AND SEA
Christopher Wordsworth, 1807–85

Christopher Wordsworth was a nephew of the poet William Wordsworth and also had poetical gifts, as his hymns reveal; but poetry was not his true bent. He was essentially an academic and at Cambridge distinguished himself by winning highest honours in both classics and mathematics.

At the early age of 29 he was appointed headmaster of Harrow, his old school. Eight years later he abandoned that turbulent life to become a canon of Westminster. He combined this with the charge of a country parish in Berkshire with the delightful name of Stanford-in-the-Vale-cum-Goosey. Here for nineteen years he peacefully pursued his scholarly and literary interests, which included the writing of his hymns. These were published in 1862 under the title of *The Holy Year*, being mainly hymns for the Christian seasons. Seven years later he was elevated to be Bishop of Lincoln, where he spent the rest of his life.

★　　★　　★

He maintained that the first duty of a hymn was to teach 'sound doctrine', and this explains why his hymns have a strong theological and biblical flavour. His best-known ones are 'Alleluia! Alleluia! hearts to heaven' (Easter), 'See the Conqueror mounts in triumph' (Ascension), and 'Gracious Spirit, Holy Ghost', written for Quinquagesima Sunday and based on 1 Corinthians 13.

His 'O Lord of heaven and earth and sea' was published as an offertory hymn, with eight stanzas. The last two, which deal specifically with almsgiving, are now commonly omitted and the remaining six make an excellent hymn of praise.

The hymn is primarily about God's manifold gifts to us rather than about our gifts to him (viz., at the offertory). But the writer's purpose is to remind us that what *we* give to God is a response to what he gives to us and should be marked by the same generous spirit.

> O Lord of heaven and earth and sea,
> To thee all praise and glory be!
> How shall we show our love to thee,
>   Who givest all?

Who givest all. This refrain in varying forms runs all through the hymn and is its keynote. Note that the God to whom we accord 'all praise and glory' is the God of the universe, Lord of heaven, earth and sea. Accordingly his gifts are on a worldwide scale. He, the giver *of* all, is also the giver *to* all. He is the supreme giver, as the Bible repeatedly affirms. For example, 'He giveth to all life and breath and all things' (Acts 17:25 AV). '. . . who giveth us richly all things to enjoy' (1 Tim. 6:17).

That being so, 'How shall we show our love to thee?' In our almsgiving is the intended answer. But in a hundred other ways, and supremely in our Christian living and service.

The stanzas that follow designate some of God's many gifts, beginning with:

> The golden sunshine, vernal air,
> Sweet flowers and fruits thy love declare;
> Where harvests ripen, thou art there,
>   Who givest all.

God's gifts in nature are the first to be dealt with. The world we live in, God's world, is full of lovely things, most of which we take for granted. How often do we thank him for the sunshine, the fresh air, the flowers (including the wild ones) and the fruits of the earth? The ripening harvests are remembered once a year, but possibly not much more often.

We go on to thank him for other gifts, this time of a more domestic and personal nature.

> For peaceful homes, and healthful days,
> For all the blessings earth displays,
> We owe thee thankfulness and praise,
>   Who givest all.

The General Thanksgiving refers to 'all the blessings of this life', but does not attempt to name them. This stanza singles out two in particular, two of the greatest.

The first is *peaceful homes*. What a marvellous blessing that is! A peaceful home in which true love reigns is worth more than a luxurious one or the grandest palace.

The other blessing is *healthful days*. Who can estimate the value of good health? Money cannot buy it, yet to be healthy in body, mind and spirit is to be rich indeed. Possibly 'healthful days' are not ours now, as they once were; but whether past or present let us thank God for them.

★   ★   ★

The hymn does not stop at giving thanks 'for all the blessings earth displays'. It now rises to a higher level and is occupied with the greatest of God's gifts.

> Thou didst not spare thine only Son,
> But gav'st him for a world undone,
> And freely with that blessèd One
>   Thou givest all.

The words are clearly based on Romans 8:32 (NIV): 'He who did not spare his own Son, but gave him up for us all –

how will he not also, along with him, graciously give us all things?' What the apostle is emphasising is that God's love is a costly, sacrificial love. The cross is the utmost revelation of that. In giving his Son to die for us he gave the gift of highest worth, and with him all other gifts are ours.

> Thou giv'st the Holy Spirit's dower,
> Spirit of life and love and power,
> And dost his sevenfold graces shower
> Upon us all.

From the Passion the hymn passes to Pentecost. The gift of the Son is all one with the gift of the Spirit, the Spirit who imparts to us 'life and love and power'. The 'sevenfold graces' which God showers upon his people are those referred to in the bishop's prayer for the candidates in the Confirmation Service, 1662: 'Daily increase in them thy manifold gifts of grace: the spirit of wisdom and under- standing; the spirit of counsel and ghostly [spiritual] strength; the spirit of knowledge and true godliness; and fill them, O Lord, with the spirit of thy holy fear, now and for ever.'

And so to the sixth stanza in which we find clear echoes of the General Thanksgiving in which we bless God 'for his inestimable love in the redemption of the world by our Lord Jesus Christ, for the means of grace, and for the hope of glory.'

> For souls redeemed, for sins forgiven,
> For means of grace and hopes of heaven,
> Father, all praise to thee be given,
> Who givest all.

19

O LOVE OF GOD, HOW STRONG AND TRUE
Horatius Bonar, 1808–89

Horatius Bonar is deservedly known as the prince of
Scottish hymn-writers. His name is to be honoured not
only for the hymns he wrote but for his work of pioneering
the singing of hymns in Scottish churches. In his day they
were wedded to the old metrical psalms: hymns were
virtually taboo. Canon John Ellerton testified to the very
remarkable change which during Bonar's lifetime passed
over the whole of Scotland in the matter of hymnody.

★　　★　　★

He began writing his hymns during his first pastorate at
Kelso. They were intended for the children of his Sunday
school who found little to interest them in the traditional
psalmody, though they were fond of the tunes. Bonar set
himself to writing new words to some of the best-known
tunes, and the success of the experiment convinced him of
the need for providing suitable hymns to be sung in church
worship.

He entered then on a task which occupied a large place in
his life. It continued on his appointment twenty-seven years
later to the Chalmers Memorial Church, Edinburgh. He
composed some 600 hymns in the course of his ministry,
among them, 'I heard the voice of Jesus say', 'Here, O my
Lord, I see thee face to face', and 'Belovèd, let us love'.

The present is one of his less-known hymns. It is probably unfamiliar to most Anglicans, but the Free Churches

have it in their hymnals and use it frequently. It was
published in 1861, entitled 'The Love of God'. It then had
ten stanzas. Six of these will be sufficient for our purpose.

> O love of God, how strong and true!
> Eternal and yet ever new;
> Uncomprehended and unbought,
> Beyond all knowledge and all thought.

This is a fine opening to the hymn. It awakens within us a
sense of wonder and praise as we think of the love of God,
'how strong and true!' Do we think often enough of the
strength of God's love? Because his love is so strong it will
never let us go; and because it is always 'true' or faithful it
will never let us down.

Again, this love has no beginning or end. It is eternal
because God is eternal and God is love. Yet it is 'ever new':
new in the sense that each day God's love becomes something of a fresh discovery as we reflect upon his goodness
and mercy. 'Uncomprehended' it is because the divine love
passes human understanding (Eph. 3:19); and 'unbought',
for we cannot purchase it at any price, yet it is God's gift to
us all.

This first stanza firmly establishes the hymn's theme.
Those that follow are all variations on the theme.

> O heavenly love, how precious still
> In days of weariness and ill,
> In nights of pain and helplessness,
> To heal, to comfort, and to bless!

Probably we all know something of 'days of weariness and
ill', as also of 'nights of pain and helplessness'; and the older
we are the more that is likely to be true. At this point the
hymn touches our life in very sensitive areas. Weariness
may be due to many things: infirmity, old age, loneliness,
sorrow, depression. 'Ill' or illness is never easy to cope with,
especially when it involves pain.

As we face such experiences, whether by day or night, the assurance of God's love is indeed 'precious still': as precious then as ever, perhaps more precious than at other times, with its power 'to heal, to comfort, and to bless'.

*   *   *

How is the love of God revealed?

> O wide-embracing, wondrous love,
> We read thee in the sky above;
> We read thee in the earth below,
> In seas that swell and streams that flow.

God's revelation of himself in nature is the first answer to our question. His love is 'wide-embracing', in fact embracing the whole of the universe, the skies, the earth and the seas. In each we can 'read' God and discern his wisdom and power. The whole of creation mirrors the Creator, as St Paul says in Romans 1:19–23.

But God's revelation of himself does not stop there. His work in redeeming man shines more brightly than in creating him, and Bonar thus continues:

> We read thee best in him who came
> To bear for us the cross of shame,
> Sent by the Father from on high
> Our life to live, our death to die.

It is 'the cross of shame' that most fully reveals the love of God. As St John puts it, 'In this is love, not that we loved God but that he loved us and sent his Son to be the expiation for our sins' (l John 4:10 RSV). The apostle thus expands the statement he made a verse or two before: 'God is love'. Precious as it is, that is not the whole gospel. It affirms no divine act for our redemption. So Archbishop William Temple rightly insisted that the heart of the gospel is not

'God is love', but 'God so loved that he *gave*'. His love is a sacrificial love. It is love in action.

This is the essence of Bonar's stanza. The Father 'from on high' sent his Son not simply to identify himself with us and live our life. Jesus came above all to identify himself with our sins and make expiation for them – 'our death to die'.

But neither his death nor ours is the end:

> We read thy power to bless and save
> E'en in the darkness of the grave;
> Still more in resurrection-light
> We read the fullness of thy might.

*   *   *

Bonar has been dealing with the theology of creation and redemption. In the final stanza theology becomes experience.

> O love of God, our shield and stay
> Through all the perils of our way;
> Eternal love, in thee we rest,
> For ever safe, for ever blest.

Here the love of God is related to our lives. It is 'our shield and stay' along life's journey. But that love is not *it*. It is *him*, the God of love, for he himself is our shield to protect us, our stay to support us. So we rest in him, the eternal love, for in him and him alone we are 'for ever safe, for ever blest'.

20

O PRAISE YE THE LORD!
Sir Henry Baker, 1821–77

This is a case of the author being as important as the hymn, perhaps even more so. The Rev. Sir Henry Williams Baker (a priest as well as a baronet) was the man to whose genius we owe the most famous English hymnal ever produced, *Hymns Ancient and Modern*. His aim was to provide a worthy and comprehensive book of hymns for use in the Church of England in place of the small and varied collections then in circulation.

Baker was appointed chairman of the committee which met in 1858 to plan the work, and thereafter he more or less took the whole project into his own hands and saw it through to completion.

More about that in a moment. First, what sort of man was he? And how did he accomplish his task?

★   ★   ★

After graduating at Trinity College, Cambridge, he was ordained in 1844. Five years later he became vicar of Monkland, a village near Leominster, where he remained for the last twenty-six years of his life. The parish was small and the duties very light. This gave him time and freedom for outside work, in his case the production of *HA&M*. It was a very considerable undertaking, but he was a man of great versatility and driving force and devoted most of his later years to the hymnal. When he died at the age of 56 he had done more than any other man for the promotion of hymnody in the Church of England.

The first edition of the book appeared in 1861. It was an immediate success and had a huge circulation. A million copies were printed every year. The same was true of the subsequent editions. And, of course, the book is still going strong today. The latest edition, 1983, still includes many of Sir Henry's hymns, among them, 'The King of love my Shepherd is', 'Lord, thy word abideth', and 'We love the place, O God'.

*   *   *

The hymn we now turn to, 'O praise ye the Lord!', is based on some verses from Psalms 148 and 150; but they are treated with a good deal of freedom and the hymn owes more to its author than to the psalmists.

> O praise ye the Lord! praise him in the height;
> Rejoice in his word, ye angels of light;
> Ye heavens adore him by whom ye were made,
> And worship before him, in brightness arrayed.

This opening stanza has as its background the first part of Psalm 148 (RSV): 'Praise the Lord . . . Praise him in the heights. Praise him, all his angels, praise him sun and moon, praise him all you shining stars. Let them praise the name of the Lord! For he commanded and they were created.'

The hymn closely follows this pattern in calling on the 'heights' to praise God – the angelic hosts and the heavenly bodies which he made. But does it not seem strange, even absurd, for the psalmist to summons inanimate nature to join in praising God?

Yet note: in doing this he recognises a personal relation between the Creator and his creation. God loves all that he has made – and 'he did not stop from loving it when he had finished making it' (Erik Routley). So in a sense inanimate nature involuntarily praises its maker by displaying its beauty and glory and might.

The praises of men of course are different, and the next stanza deals with these as it comes down to earth.

O praise ye the Lord! praise him upon earth,
In tuneful accord, ye sons of new birth;
Praise him who hath brought you his grace from above,
Praise him who hath taught you to sing of his love.

The psalm ends by leaving behind the world of nature and concentrating on the human family, and more especially on the people of God: 'He has raised up a horn for his people, praise for all his saints, for the people of Israel who are near to him. Praise the Lord!' (v. 14 RSV). Accordingly Sir Henry Baker now writes of the people of God: not the Jewish people but the people of the new covenant, the people of Christ.

So there is now a change of language. In moving out of the Old Testament into the New the writer gives the hymn a distinctly Christian flavour. Those here called upon to render praise are 'the sons of new birth', those who have been born again by water and the Spirit (John 3:5). These are the recipients of God's grace which in Christ has appeared for their salvation (Titus 2:11); and in response they 'sing of his love'. How could they fail to do so?

★   ★   ★

The third stanza is based on the part of Psalm 150 (vv. 3–5) which calls us to praise God to the music of trumpet and cymbals, lute and harp, strings and pipe.

O praise ye the Lord, all things that give sound;
Each jubilant chord re-echo around;
Loud organs, his glory forth tell in deep tone,
And, sweet harp, the story of what he hath done.

The psalmist's orchestra must have given 'sound' all right, but the music which Sir Henry Baker had in mind was of a

more melodious nature. He refers to the deep tone of the
organ and the sweet notes of the harp which accompany our
songs as we praise God for what he has done.

For most of us, if not for all, music is an essential part of
our worship. Without it the praises we offer would be poor
indeed. It is both our duty and delight to make a joyful noise
to the Lord with songs of praise (Ps. 95:2).

★   ★   ★

So to the final stanza.

> O praise ye the Lord! thanksgiving and song
> To him be outpoured all ages along;
> For love in creation, for heaven restored,
> For grace of salvation, O praise ye the Lord!

What a splendid paean of praise! It perfectly matches the
spirit of the whole hymn and rounds it off on a note of
triumph. 'Thanksgiving and song' are to be outpoured to
the Lord both now and throughout all ages: for his love
manifested in the work of creation, for his grace revealed in
the yet greater work of salvation, and for thus opening to us
sinners the door of heaven.

O praise ye the Lord indeed!

21

PRAISE, MY SOUL, THE KING OF HEAVEN
Henry Francis Lyte, 1793–1847

In a book of this kind it would scarcely be possible to omit Lyte's magnificent hymn of praise. It is one of the best-known hymns ever written and has become a great national favourite. On November 20th, 1947, exactly a hundred years after Lyte's death, Princess (now Queen) Elizabeth chose it to be sung at her wedding in Westminster Abbey.

Some credit for the hymn's immense popularity must doubtless be given to Sir John Goss (1800–80) who composed for it the tune *Praise my Soul* to which it is now almost invariably sung. But our concern is with the words, not with the tune. Before we look at them let us find out something about the man who wrote them.

★　　★　　★

The name of Henry Francis Lyte is associated with Brixham on the south coast of Devon. It was here that he came as a young clergyman in 1823 to take charge of the newly-formed parish, then a small fishing village. It was here he remained for the rest of his life, and it was here he wrote his many poems and hymns, the last of them being 'Abide with me'.

But we must go back to the beginning of his story. Though born of English parents, he spent most of his early life in Ireland and graduated at Trinity College, Dublin. For three successive years he won the University's prize for an English poem. Ordained in 1815, he soon afterwards left

Ireland to serve a curacy at Marazion in Cornwall. Here he experienced a deep evangelical conversion which transformed his life and ministry.

At Brixham he published several books of religious verse, the most important being *The Spirit of the Psalms*, 1834. It was a collection of 280 hymns based on the Psalms, but not simply paraphrases of them. Lyte's concern was to penetrate their spiritual message and express it in a poetical form suitable for Christian worship. 'Praise my soul' was his treatment of Psalm 103 and his masterpiece. It consisted of five stanzas, of which four are now in general use. In the fifth line of each Lyte wrote 'Praise him! Praise him!' Some books now change this to a double 'Alleluia', but the meaning is the same.

★   ★   ★

> Praise, my soul, the King of heaven,
>   To his feet thy tribute bring;
> Ransomed, healed, restored, forgiven,
>   Who like me his praise should sing?

This first stanza covers the first five verses of the psalm, which begins: 'Praise the Lord, O my soul, and all that is within me praise his holy name. Praise the Lord, O my soul, and forget not all his benefits' (Ps. 103:1–2 BCP). The praise here is personal and the hymn accordingly begins on the same note. *My* soul must praise the Lord. I must bring my own grateful tribute to the King of heaven. And there is a reason for this: I must 'forget not all his benefits'.

The psalm states some of those benefits (vv. 3–5). The hymn sums them up in four memorable words: 'Ransomed, healed, restored, forgiven'. In picture language they express four different aspects of our salvation.

Ransomed is concerned with liberation, freedom.

Healed is about wholeness, health of mind and body.

Restored means the renewal of our spiritual vigour, making us 'young and lusty as an eagle' (BCP).

Forgiven, though listed last, is the first of all the Lord's
    benefits, as in the psalm.
Forget not *all* his benefits? We can't remember even a
fraction of them!
The next stanza, like the psalm, takes a wider sweep. Not
the individual but the Lord's people are now in view.

> Praise him for his grace and favour
>   To our fathers in distress;

Who were they, 'our fathers in distress'? The psalm supplies
the answer: 'The Lord executeth righteousness and judgment to all that are oppressed. He made known his ways
unto Moses, his acts unto the children of Israel' (vv. 6,7
AV).

The mention of Moses identifies the historical occasion.
In Egypt the enslaved Israelites are cruelly oppressed. In his
'grace and favour' God raises up his servant to be their
deliverer. The people witness the Lord's works of judgment
and are emancipated, free to journey to the promised
land.

The New Testament sees in this narrative a picture of the
redeeming work of Christ for his people. It also teaches us
today to look back into history and remember what the
Lord has done for his Church in times of oppression and
persecution, that we may

> Praise him, still the same for ever,
>   Slow to chide, and swift to bless.

The psalm says at this point that the Lord is merciful and
gracious and will not always chide (vv. 8,9). The hymn
goes further and says that not only is he 'slow to chide' but
also 'swift to bless', a gracious addition to the psalmist's
words.

★   ★   ★

The third stanza continues the theme of God's dealings with his people, as in the psalm: 'As a father pities his children, so the Lord pities those who fear him. For he knows our frame; he remembers that we are but dust' (vv. 13,14 RSV). This surely is one of the tenderest passages in the Psalms, if not in the entire Old Testament. And Lyte beautifully matches both its spirit and its language:

> Father-like, he tends and spares us;
>   Well our feeble frame he knows;
> In his hands he gently bears us,
>   Rescues us from all our foes.

The concept of the fatherhood of God is not often found in the Old Testament. He is thought of rather as Creator, King and Judge, and of course he is. But he is something more. Jesus unveiled to us the ultimate truth about God and taught us to think of him as our loving, heavenly Father, and as such to trust him and pray to him.

The Psalm ends by affirming God's universal kingship and calling on all creation to join with us in praising him (vv. 19–22). The hymn's last stanza echoes this.

> Angels, help us to adore him,
>   Ye behold him face to face;
> Sun and moon, bow down before him,
>   Dwellers all in time and space.
>   Alleluia! Alleluia!
>   Praise with us the God of grace.

Like the psalm the hymn concludes on a note of universal praise. It asserts that everybody and everything must pay homage to the Lord: the angels who behold him face to face, the created order above and around us, and the whole of humanity. That includes each of us personally; and so the psalmist ends his song in the same way that he began it: 'Praise thou the Lord, O *my* soul!'

22

PRAISE THE LORD! YE HEAVENS ADORE HIM
Foundling Hospital Collection, 1796

You will see that this hymn has a strange ascription: 'Foundling Hospital Collection, 1796'. It is doubtful whether the words convey any meaning to those who sing the hymn, or whether they have ever taken the trouble to find out. More's the pity, for behind the words is a most interesting piece of English social history of the eighteenth century.

The history is certainly worth exploring. Among other things it reminds us that social conditions and needs in the England of nearly two centuries ago were not altogether unlike those of our own day.

★   ★   ★

The Foundling Hospital in High Holborn, London, was an orphanage for destitute and abandoned children. It was one of many such institutions that sprang up in the wake of the Methodist Revival. The founder was Thomas Coram, a retired captain of the Merchant Navy.

On arriving at St Andrew's, Holborn, one Sunday morning he found an abandoned baby lying on the church steps. He and his wife were childless, so they took the baby home and cared for it. Coram later discovered that there were many such babies in London, abandoned and left to die. His compassion was stirred and he resolved to found a home to meet this tragic need. An appeal for funds met with a wonderfully generous response and as a result the 'Hospital' was soon established and became the means of saving thousands of children's lives.

The children were well looked after and given a good education. What is of particular interest to us is that they were all taught to sing. In fact, their singing attracted public attention and became a feature of London life. Fashionable people used to attend the Sunday services to listen to the children singing their hymns. Handel became deeply interested and not only presented an organ to the chapel but each year conducted a special performance of *Messiah* to raise money for the work.

In view of all this it is hardly surprising that the Hospital had its own collection of hymns, published in 1796, and the present hymn comes from that collection.

★   ★   ★

The hymn is worth looking at. Nothing is known of its authorship, but it was headed 'Hymn from Psalm 148, Haydn'. This tells us something about both the words and the music. The words are based on Psalm 148, and it was sung to Haydn's celebrated tune *Austria* with which it is still associated.

The psalm begins with 'Praise the Lord', or in Hebrew 'Hallelujah' (*hallelu* – praise; *Jah* – the Lord). That word was a feature of Jewish worship. The psalter rings with it. And it has since entered deeply into our Christian worship, for praise is at the heart of it all. True praise – that is giving glory to God in the highest and losing ourselves in his majesty and power – is fundamental not only to worship but to life itself. Man never rises to a greater height than when he bows at the Lord's feet in selfless adoration.

The whole of Psalm 148 is praise. In particular the first twelve verses call upon the whole creation to unite in praising God, as does the first stanza of the hymn.

> Praise the Lord! ye heavens adore him;
> Praise him, angels, in the height;

Sun and moon, rejoice before him,
  Praise him, all ye stars and light.
Praise the Lord! for he hath spoken;
  Worlds his mighty voice obeyed:
Laws, which never shall be broken,
  For their guidance he hath made.

Compare the language of the hymn with the verses of the psalm and you will see how closely they correspond. Thus 'ye heavens adore him' is derived from verse 1; 'praise him, angels in the height' (v. 2); 'sun and moon, rejoice before him' (v. 3a); 'praise him, all ye stars and light' (v. 3b); 'praise the Lord, for he hath spoken' (v. 5); 'worlds his mighty voice obeyed; (v. 5); and 'laws which never shall be broken' (v. 6).

So much for the first six verses of the psalm. What about the next six, beginning 'Praise the Lord upon earth'? We might have expected them to be the substance of the second stanza, but they are not. That stanza, as we shall see, follows a different course.

The probable reason is that the verses of the psalm do not lend themselves to poetical treatment. A glance at the words will show that this is true. Nevertheless it would have been good to have an allusion to the twelfth verse, especially in a children's hymn: 'Both . . . young men and maidens, old men and children, let them praise the name of the Lord' (v. 12 AV).

*   *   *

We now look at the second stanza. It contains some echoes of the psalm but is not directly related to it like the other. It goes further and soars higher. It turns from the created order to *people*: God's people and God's dealings with them.

Praise the Lord! for he is glorious;
  Never shall his promise fail;

> God hath made his saints victorious;
>   Sin and death shall not prevail.
> Praise the God of our salvation;
>   Hosts on high his power proclaim;
> Heaven and earth and all creation
>   Laud and magnify his name!

It has been suggested that the stanza draws its inspiration from the final verse of the psalm: 'He shall exalt the horn of his people: all his saints shall praise him, even the children of Israel, a people near unto him. Praise the Lord!'

Naturally the references in the psalm are to the Jewish people, the children of Israel. The hymn, quite rightly, has a broader vision. It leads us out of the Old Testament into the New. The glorious God whom we praise is the God and Father of our Lord Jesus Christ. The 'saints' who are victorious are the blessed company of all believers. 'Sin and death shall not prevail' because of Christ's redemptive work. By his Cross he paid the price of sin and by his Resurrection he vanquished death.

So with the hosts on high we 'praise the God of our salvation', while

> Heaven and earth and all creation
> Laud and magnify his name.

23

PRAISE TO THE LORD, THE ALMIGHTY, THE KING OF CREATION
Joachim Neander, 1650–80,
trs. Catherine Winkworth, 1827–78

This magnificent hymn of praise comes from Germany, the homeland of hymn-singing as we know it today. For it all began with Luther and the Reformation. Before that time hymns were sung only in the monasteries, and then all in Latin. The ordinary people had no share in them. Luther changed that situation. He wanted the people to sing of their new-found faith and not only wrote hymns himself but encouraged others to do so. As a result more hymns have probably been written in German than in any other language.

This hymn, and also its tune, date from more than 300 years ago. Our English translation is the work of Miss Catherine Winkworth.

★   ★   ★

Joachim Neander's life was short but by no means uneventful. Both his father and grandfather were Lutheran pastors, but at first he showed no signs of following in their steps. His student days in Bremen were spent in riotous living. But when he was about 20 a famous Pietist (Evangelical) preacher named Under-Eyke came to the town and under his preaching Neander was converted. At once he dedicated his life to Christ's service and became a lay pastor in the Lutheran Church.

Some difficult years followed. At an early age he was appointed principal of the Latin School in Dusseldorf; but his strong pietistic views and evangelistic activities displeased the church authorities and he was obliged to resign. Soon afterwards his health deteriorated and he returned to his home town of Bremen. Here he fell victim to consumption and died at the age of 30.

A brief life indeed, but in those last ten years he achieved much, especially through his hymns. Most of them, some sixty in all, were written at Dusseldorf, and these are the abiding legacy he left to the Church.

★   ★   ★

Each of the hymn's four stanzas has its particular character.

> Praise to the Lord, the Almighty, the King of Creation!
> O my soul praise him, for he is thy health and
>   salvation.
>   Come ye, who hear,
>   Brothers and sisters draw near,
> Praise him in glad adoration!

'The King of *creation*' – that is the word to note here. God is the Creator, the Maker of heaven and earth, and as such he is worthy of all praise.

Neander was a great nature-lover. During his Dusseldorf days he found release from the burdens of life by taking long rambles in the surrounding valleys and holding communion with God amid the works of his hands. He discovered in the beauty and majesty of nature a revelation of God's love and a source of healing power. This imparts a special meaning to the line, 'O my soul praise him, for he is thy health and salvation.' The words *health* and *salvation* are closely related. They both have to do with wholeness: soundness of body, mind and spirit (see 1 Thess. 5:23).

Praise to the Lord, who o'er all things so
        wondrously reigneth!
Shelters thee under his wings, yea, so gently
        sustaineth.
  Hast thou not seen?
  All that is needful hath been
Granted in what he ordaineth.

The sovereignty of God is the note that sounds out in this
second stanza. We give praise to the Lord 'who o'er all
things so wondrously reigneth!' But is that true? Is God
really sovereign over all and responsible for everything that
happens in life?

The question brings us face to face with the mystery of
divine providence. And mystery it is. As Christians we
believe that God is in command of the human situation, but
many things happen in life that we cannot understand or
explain. Nevertheless, we accept the apostle's words that 'in
everything God works for good with those who love him'
(Rom. 8:28 RSV), or in the words of the hymn that what in
his sovereign will he 'ordaineth' (note that word) is ulti-
mately the fulfilment of his loving purposes for his people.

★   ★   ★

Our praise continues in a somewhat more personal strain.

Praise to the Lord who doth prosper thy work and
        defend thee!
Surely his goodness and mercy here daily attend thee.
  Ponder anew
  What the Almighty can do,
He who with love doth befriend thee.

God is our refuge and strength, says the psalmist, a very
present help in trouble (Ps. 46:1 AV). That is the thought
here, and it brings God very near to us in daily life. He is

always close at hand. He sees what we are doing, prospers our work, and defends us in time of danger.

And so to the end he 'befriends' us – a lovely thought. The God whom we praise in this hymn is not only the Almighty Lord, the King, the Creator. He is also our friend, and that brings him closer to us still.

Adoration is the keynote of the final stanza, which contains echoes of Psalms 103 and 150.

> Praise to the Lord! O let all that is in me adore him!
> All that hath life and breath come now with praises
>   before him!
>   Let the amen
>   Sound from his people again:
> Gladly for ay we adore him.

Note the two *alls* in this verse. First, 'let all that is in me adore him!' The words recall Psalm 103:1, 'Praise the Lord, O my soul, and all that is within me praise his holy name'. Next, 'All that hath life and breath come now with praises before him.' Psalm 150:6 is in mind here: 'Let everything that has breath praise the Lord!' So the 'amen' sounds from every heart, and gladly, for ever, *we* adore him.

★   ★   ★

The English translation of this hymn, as already mentioned, was made by Miss Catherine Winkworth (1827–78), a woman of brilliant intellect, who translated nearly 400 German hymns into English and earned the title of queen of translators. Among her other hymns is 'Now thank we all our God' (Chapter 17). In later life she worked hard for the higher education of women and helped in founding University College, Bristol – now the University.

24

REJOICE, THE LORD IS KING
Charles Wesley, 1707–88

It is rather surprising to discover that this famous hymn by Charles Wesley comes from his collection of *Hymns for our Lord's Resurrection*, 1746. It is not normally associated with Easter, for it contains no actual reference to the risen Jesus or the empty tomb. On the other hand, it abounds in references to the Lord's exaltation into heaven and his kingly throne and is thus an ideal hymn for Ascensiontide. What are we to say to that?

The most probable answer is that in the New Testament the resurrection and ascension of our Lord are closely linked, especially in the fourth Gospel. Both celebrate his exaltation. In his resurrection he was raised from death to life. In his ascension he was raised from earth to heaven. The risen Christ is the reigning Christ.

★　　★　　★

We look now at Wesley's hymn, and first at its refrain:

> *Lift up your heart, lift up your voice;*
> *Rejoice; again I say, Rejoice.*

The refrain is one of the features of the hymn. It is derived from two sources, ancient liturgy and Holy Scripture. 'Lift up your heart' comes from the *Sursum corda* in the Eucharist (see Chapter 14). To this call Wesley adds another: 'Lift up your voice' (*cf*. Isa. 40:9). The heart and the voice – how well they go together! No doubt to lift up the heart in worship is more important than to lift up the voice; but we cannot use the voice better than to lift it up with our hearts to praise and magnify the Lord.

The second part of the refrain is based on St Paul's words in Philippians 4:4, 'Rejoice in the Lord alway; again I say, rejoice' (AV). At the time he wrote, his readers were suffering persecution for their faith. But note: he bids them to rejoice not in their circumstances but *in the Lord*.

Wesley's original hymn had six stanzas. One of these has now dropped out of use. Of the remaining five, many books print only four, but we shall look at the five to make the hymn complete. It is saturated, like nearly all Wesley's hymns, with biblical allusions; and although it might seem to be largely repetitive, the repetition is not monotonous. Wesley skilfully builds up his theme, adds fresh material, and holds our interest throughout. Let us see how.

> Rejoice, the Lord is King!
>   Your Lord and King adore;
> Mortals, give thanks and sing,
>   And triumph evermore.

Rejoice – the keynote of the hymn. Our joy is centred on the living Christ, now the King of glory. Three other responses are suggested on our part.

Adoration – 'Your Lord and King adore.' This is the response of worship.

Thanksgiving – 'Mortals, give thanks and sing'. Not just silent thanksgiving, you will observe, but the kind that expresses itself in song.

Exultation – 'And triumph evermore.' Our exultation derives from Christ's exaltation.

The next stanza continues the theme.

> Jesus the Saviour reigns,
>   The God of truth and love;
> When he had purged our stains,
>   He took his seat above.

If you look at it carefully you will see that this stanza tells us a lot about Jesus: five things in fact. First, his *saviourhood*, for that is what his name Jesus means (Matt. 1:21). Next, his *sovereignty*, for he 'reigns' and reigns now. Third, his *deity*: he is 'the God of truth and love'. Fourth, his *atonement*: 'When he had purged our stains,' for he did that by the shedding of his blood. And fifth, his *enthronement*: 'he took his seat above.'

Wesley compresses some strong theology into just four lines and leads us from the cross to the throne. The last two lines are a paraphrase of a verse from the Epistle to the Hebrews in which the writer says of Jesus: 'When he had made purification for sins, he sat down at the right hand of the Majesty on high' (1:3 RSV).

★   ★   ★

The next two stanzas continue to dwell on the kingship of Jesus.

> His kingdom cannot fail,
>   He rules o'er earth and heaven;
> The keys of death and hell
>   Are to our Jesus given.

The kingship of Jesus is inevitably linked with his kingdom. Probably Wesley was thinking here of the passage in Revelation 11:15, made familiar to us in Handel's *Messiah*: 'The kingdoms of the world are become the kingdom of our Lord and of his Christ, and he shall reign for ever and ever' (AV).

Christ's reign is worldwide and eternal; it also extends over the unseen world, as the last two lines affirm. Again we are in the book of Revelation. The apostle sees a glowing vision of the risen Lord who says, '. . . I am the first and the last and the living one; I died, and behold I am alive for evermore, and I have the keys of death and Hades' (1:17–8 RSV). The keys are the symbol of authority. Because Jesus died and now lives for ever he has power not only over death but over Hades or 'hell', the place of the departed.

> He sits at God's right hand,
> Till all his foes submit,
> And bow to his command,
> And fall beneath his feet.

This stanza draws its inspiration from 1 Corinthians 15:24,25: 'Then comes the end, when he [Jesus] delivers the kingdom to God the Father . . . For he must reign until he has put all his enemies under his feet' (RSV). The words point to the final consummation, the climax of history, the triumphant fulfilment of God's ultimate purposes for mankind.

Hence the final stanza:

> Rejoice in glorious hope;
> Jesus the Judge shall come,
> And take his servants up
> To their eternal home.

Many hymnals omit these words, yet without them the hymn as Wesley planned it is incomplete. More important still, without them the gospel itself is incomplete. The coming of the Lord to take his servants to their eternal home is the final chapter of the good news which the apostles preached. See, for example, 1 Thessalonians 4:13–17, which also provides the material of the hymn's last refrain:

> *We soon shall hear the archangel's voice,*
> *The trump of God shall sound, Rejoice!*

*   *   *

A final word must be added about the hymn's famous tune, one of three which Handel composed for Wesley's hymns. For some reason these tunes were lost sight of after Wesley's

death. Then in 1826 his son Samuel, a well-known
musician, discovered them in Handel's handwriting in the
library of the Fitzwilliam Museum at Cambridge. The
composer had named this one *Gopsal*: the home of his friend
Charles Jenner, near Ashby-de-la-Zouch. It was Jenner
who compiled the libretto for the *Messiah*.

25

SONGS OF PRAISE THE ANGELS SANG
James Montgomery, 1771–1854

It is questionable whether the name of James Montgomery is familiar to most church people. Yet it is a name of considerable importance in the story of English hymnody. Dr Routley ranked Montgomery next to Watts and Wesley among English hymn-writers, a high honour indeed. He is almost certainly the finest of English lay hymn-writers.

A man of immense literary gifts, he achieved in his day a high reputation as a poet. He felt the urge to write poetry while still at school and hoped to make this his career. But the struggle was a hard one and he later turned to journalism. For thirty years he was editor of a Sheffield newspaper. Throughout his long life he continued to write an immense amount of verse and prose; but when in old age he was asked by a friend which of his poems would survive, he replied, 'None, sir, except perhaps a few of my hymns.'

So it has proved. Many of his 400 hymns are still in regular use. Among them are 'Stand up and bless the Lord', 'Angels from the realms of glory', 'Lord, teach us how to pray aright', 'For ever with the Lord', and what is regarded as his greatest, 'Hail to the Lord's Anointed'.

*   *   *

His hymns maintain a consistently high level and 'Songs of praise the angels sang' (published 1819) is typical of his work. It adheres closely to its theme, it is biblical in its teaching, and it follows a clear, orderly pattern. The first three stanzas celebrate God's work in creation and redemption, while the last three are concerned with the Church's praise in response to what God has done.

> Songs of praise the angels sang,
> Heaven with alleluias rang,
> When creation was begun,
> When God spake and it was done.

Songs of praise. The three words have given their name to the famous hymn-book first published in 1926 and to the BBC's popular television programme. Here the recurrent phrase epitomises the hymn's entire theme and gives it both unity and strength.

This first stanza is about creation. It takes us back to the opening words of the Bible, 'In the beginning God created the heavens and the earth . . . And God said, Let there be light, and there was light.' Thus the hymn: 'God spake and it was done', for his Word has creative power (see Ps. 33:9).

When this happened 'Songs of praise the angels sang', says the hymn. The reference is probably to the poetic description of creation in the Book of Job when 'the morning stars sang together, and all the sons of God shouted for joy' (38:7 AV). The sons of God are commonly taken to be the angels.

The hymn passes from God's creative to his redemptive work, wrought in the coming of Christ.

> Songs of praise awoke the morn
> When the Prince of Peace was born;
> Songs of praise arose when he
> Captive led captivity.

When Montgomery published his hymn he gave it the title 'Glory to God in the Highest'. Here then is the multitude of the heavenly host with their songs of praise on the first Christmas morning 'when the Prince of Peace was born' (Luke 2:8–14). It is always good to remember that Christianity began with an outburst of song, and *Gloria in excelsis Deo* remains the keynote of the Church's worship.

The Incarnation, however, is not the whole gospel. The purpose of Christ's coming to earth was to save men from their sins, to break the power of evil and overcome death; and this redeeming work he accomplished by his passion and resurrection crowned by his exaltation when he ascended on high and led a host of captives (Eph. 4:8). This is another theme for songs of praise. Christ is the conqueror who having completed his work on earth now reigns in heaven.

The third stanza goes further and points to the final chapter in the story of man's redemption.

> Heaven and earth must pass away,
> Songs of praise shall crown that day;
> God will make new heavens and earth,
> Songs of praise shall hail their birth.

What do we know about the dissolution of heaven and earth, the winding up of the present order, the creation of God's new world? Little indeed. Nothing in fact but what is revealed in the Scriptures. Montgomery knows this and does not indulge in speculation. He turns to the Book of Revelation, the Apocalypse, a word meaning the unveiling. And what an unveiling is here!

> Then I saw a new heaven and a new earth, for the first heaven and the first earth had passed away . . . And he who sat on the throne said, 'Behold, I make all things new' (21:1,5, RSV).

★   ★   ★

In the last three stanzas our songs of praise continue on a different level, in the worship of the Church on earth.

> And shall man alone be dumb
> Till that glorious kingdom come?

> No! the Church delights to raise
> Psalms and hymns and songs of praise.

The praises of the heavenly hosts present a challenge to us.
'Shall man alone be dumb?' Can we remain silent while we
await the coming of the great day of God? The question is
answered by a decisive 'No!' The Church delights to emu-
late the angels and give glory to God in the highest. From
the beginning this has been characteristic of Christ's
Church. It has always been a singing Church, praising God
in 'psalms and hymns and spiritual songs' (Eph. 5:19). And
so it remains today:

> Saints below, with heart and voice,
> Still in songs of praise rejoice,
> Learning here, by faith and love,
> Songs of praise to sing above.

God's *saints* – by which is meant the whole company of his
people – seldom meet together in worship without raising
their voices in song, whether it be in a magnificent cathedral
or a humble village chapel. All such singing is equally
acceptable to God, provided it be 'with heart and voice' –
and not with the voice alone. And Montgomery suggests
that such singing is the prelude to, and preparation for, the
worship of the Church in heaven.

The final stanza tells us something more about the singing of the saints:

> Borne upon their latest breath,
> Songs of praise shall conquer death;
> Then, amidst eternal joy,
> Songs of praise their powers employ.

This, Montgomery's original stanza, affirms one simple
truth. For the people of God the ministry of song never
ceases, whether in life or death, whether on earth or in
heaven.

26

TELL OUT, MY SOUL, THE GREATNESS OF THE LORD
Timothy Dudley-Smith (b. 1926)

This is the only hymn by a contemporary author included among these hymns of praise. No one will question its right to be there. Though written less than thirty years ago, it has become a firm favourite and has sung its way round the world.

The late Sir John Betjeman, the Poet Laureate, described it in 1976 as 'one of the few new hymns really to have established themselves in recent years.' There has certainly been no lack of new hymns in the last two or three decades, but time alone will tell how many of them will survive. This one has already passed the test and in many ways stands in a class by itself.

★   ★   ★

It is not necessary to give more than a sketch of the author's life to date.

Timothy Dudley-Smith was educated at Tonbridge and Cambridge and ordained in the Rochester diocese in 1950. Since 1981 he has been Bishop of Thetford in the diocese of Norwich. Before that he was Archdeacon of Norwich for eight years. Much of his earlier ministry was spent in the service of the Church Pastoral-Aid Society as assistant and then as general secretary. During that time he extended the publishing side of the Society's work. He also had a large part in the production of *Psalm Praise*, 1973, to which he contributed some twenty hymns.

His collected works were published in 1984 under the title of *Lift Every Heart*. 'Tell out my soul' was one of his earliest hymns, written in May 1961. He tells how at the time he was reading the Magnificat – the song of the Virgin Mary (Luke 1:46–55) – in the New English Bible, then recently published. He was struck by the opening words, 'Tell out, my soul, the greatness of the Lord,' which at once suggested themselves to him as the first line of a hymn. He set to work on the idea and the result was this fine metrical version of the famous canticle. For many people it has made Mary's Magnificat come alive in a new way.

Much of the phraseology of the New English Bible text is woven into the hymn, and this provides the cue to the four stanzas.

*   *   *

Tell out, my soul, the greatness of the Lord;
    Unnumbered blessings, give my spirit voice;
Tender to me the promise of his word;
    In God my Saviour shall my heart rejoice.

As we all know, the earlier versions of Mary's song begin 'My soul doth *magnify* the Lord'. To magnify is to make great or greater and this probably suggested to the NEB translators the phrase 'the greatness of the Lord'. At any rate we need to think a lot about his greatness. However small an idea we may have of ourselves, we cannot have too great an idea of God.

Mary was rejoicing in the Lord's greatness throughout her song and to begin with in what he had done for her personally, 'humble as she is' (Like 1:48). For of all women in the world he had chosen her to be the mother of the promised Messiah. She nowhere refers directly to God's gift to her, the precious Life conceived within her womb; but this is the essential meaning of her words, 'so tenderly has he looked upon his servant'. The hymn beautifully echoes these words, and the Virgin's exultant spirit is reflected in the line, 'In God my Saviour shall my heart rejoice.'

Each stanza of the hymn begins by referring to the Lord's greatness. Thus the second:

Tell out, my soul, the greatness of his name:
   Make known his might, the deeds his arm has done;
His mercy sure, from age to age the same;
   His holy name, the Lord, the Mighty One.

Let us begin here by noting two sentences from Mary's song. The first is: 'his mercy sure from generation to generation towards those who fear him' (v. 50). The second: 'the deeds his own right arm has done disclose his might' (v. 51).

These words are the substance of this stanza. Clearly it deals with the same two themes, God's mercy and his might, but in the reverse order. First then, 'Make known his might, the deeds his arm has done'. The Lord's 'arm' in the Bible is the symbol of his saving power, as for example in the song of Moses (Exod. 15) when he praises God for delivering his people from Egypt 'by the greatness of thine arm'. As Christians we praise him for the greater deliverance wrought for us in Jesus Christ.

But closely linked with the Lord's might is 'his mercy sure, from age to age the same'. In her song Mary has no thought of her own goodness or worthiness. She is mindful only of God's mercy to her, and that mercy is unchanging in every age.

★   ★   ★

The central part of the Magnificat (vv. 51–3) looks forward to the coming of God's kingdom, or kingly rule, through the birth of the Messiah. This is how the hymn expresses it.

Tell out, my soul, the greatness of his might;
   Powers and dominions lay their glory by;

> Proud hearts and stubborn wills are put to flight,
>   The hungry fed, the humble lifted high.

The words are a poetic description of the new order of
society which Christ is to establish: a society in which the
proud will be humiliated, the mighty overthrown, the
lowly exalted, the hungry satisfied. Incidentally, at this
point the Magnificat bears close resemblances to the song of
Hannah in 1 Samuel 2 (e.g. vv. 3–8).

The picture is revolutionary, for the gospel of the kingdom is a revolutionary message. Where God's rule is acknowledged and Christ is owned as king something
tremendous happens. Society is transformed, new stan-
dards are established, and men and women are changed into
the sort of people God intends them to be.

In the last strains of her song Mary looks back to the past
and says in effect 'God is faithful to his promise.' The
hymn's final stanza says the same.

> Tell out, my soul, the glories of his word:
>   Firm is his promise, and his mercy sure.
> Tell out, my soul, the greatness of the Lord
>   To children's children and for evermore.

The promise in question is God's promise to Abraham
and the Jewish forefathers concerning the coming of the
Messiah. Mary sees that this will be fulfilled through the
birth of her son, for God has 'not forgotten to show mercy
to Abraham and his children's children, for ever' (v. 55).

In keeping with this the hymn ends by affirming God's
mercy and faithfulness and 'the glories of his word'. That
word of promise, spoken long centuries past to Israel, is
now realised in the person of Christ and the people of Christ
in his worldwide Church.

27

THE LORD IS KING! LIFT UP
THY VOICE
Josiah Conder, 1789–1855

Although the name of Josiah Conder is little known today,
he was quite a notable figure in the world of hymnody at the
beginning of the last century. A true Londoner (born at
Aldersgate, died at Hampstead) he was the son of an
engraver and bookseller and at the age of 13 entered his
father's business. Despite his lack of educational advan-
tages, he had marked literary ability. In the course of his life
he wrote a considerable number of hymns and published
several volumes of poetry. His verse was commended by
Robert Southey, then Poet Laureate.

A leading Congregational layman of his day, in 1836 he
edited the church's first official hymn-book. This included
some sixty of his own compositions. Not many of these are
now in use, even in the Free Churches. Probably the most
widely known is 'Bread of heaven, on thee we feed', a
communion hymn of a deeply devotional character.

★   ★   ★

'The Lord is King' is a very different sort of hymn. It was
published in Conder's *Star of the East*, 1824, and headed with
the text: 'Alleluia! for the Lord God omnipotent reigneth'
(Rev. 19:6 AV). The text – repeated in the final stanza – is
from the New Testament, but the hymn as a whole has an
Old Testament ring about it. The phrase 'The Lord is King'
comes straight from the Psalms. Many of them begin with
the words, often translated 'The Lord reigns!' For example:

'The Lord reigns! Let the earth be glad, let the distant shores rejoice' (Ps. 97:1 NIV).

'The Lord reigns! Let the nations tremble! He sits enthroned between the cherubim' (Ps. 99:1 NIV).

'Say among the nations, "The Lord reigns!"' (Ps. 96:10 NIV).

All these quotations stress the universality of God's kingship. He reigns over all the earth, among all nations. This note, which sounds all through the hymn, is heard in the first stanza:

> The Lord is King! lift up thy voice,
> O earth, and all ye heavens rejoice;
> From world to world the joy shall ring,
> 'The Lord omnipotent is King!'

The sovereignty of God is an essential Bible truth, and his sovereignty is unlimited. He is no local monarch. The whole world is under his sway. And he is King *now*. He has never abdicated his throne and never will. The nations and the individuals within them may or may not recognise his sovereignty. They are free to choose. In any case it does not alter the fact. The difference is this. To reject his rule is to come under his judgment. To accept it is to enjoy the peace and security of his kingdom.

What of ourselves? It is one thing to acknowledge the truth of God's sovereignty and to sing with great enthusiasm 'Our God reigns!' But how does this truth affect *us*? That is the question the hymn proceeds to answer.

For one thing it scatters our doubts and fears.

> The Lord is King! who then shall dare
> Resist his will, distrust his care,
> Or murmur at his wise decrees,
> Or doubt his royal promises?

The Lord who is King of all the earth cares for each one of his children and is utterly trustworthy. There are times and occasions when we may be tempted to doubt that, for his ways are often hidden from us and life is full of perplexing things which we cannot explain.

But come what may – and mercifully the future is unknown to us – we must believe that God's will is good and perfect, that his loving care for us never ceases, and that his 'decrees' or purposes are always wise. And then there are his promises – his 'royal promises' the hymn calls them, for they are the promises of a king. To distrust them is not only presumption but folly, for it is to deprive ourselves of the joy and peace which are ours in believing.

★   ★   ★

All this is expressed in other words in the third stanza.

> The Lord is King! child of the dust
> The Judge of all the earth is just;
> Holy and true are all his ways;
> Let every creature speak his praise.

The King is also the Judge, and a just one. In writing this Conder was thinking of the words of Abraham, 'Shall not the Judge of all the earth do right?' (Gen. 18:25). There is great comfort to be had in those words, especially when things seem to go wrong. In our earthliness as 'children of dust' we may sometimes think that the judge of all the earth is unjust rather than just. But of one thing we may be sure. God will never do wrong, never be unjust, never act contrary to his nature of love. 'Holy and just are all his ways', which simply means that he reigns in righteousness.

> He reigns! ye saints, exalt your strains;
> Your God is King, your Father reigns;
> And he is at the Father's side,
> The Man of love, the Crucified.

Another factor emerges here. 'Your God is King' we already know; but there is something more: 'your *Father* reigns'. Our King and our Judge is also our Father. That brings God nearer to us. Not only does he reign in right-eousness (he could do no other) but he reigns in love as well. He is truly the King of love.

To enforce this fact we have the only reference in the hymn to the Lord Jesus Christ, 'the Man of love, the Crucified'. He who became man for us and died for us is now exalted to the right hand of the Father as our advocate, mediator, and high priest.

★   ★   ★

The two final stanzas bring us back to the truth of God's *universal* kingship.

> Alike pervaded by his eye
> All parts of his dominion lie:
> This world of ours and worlds unseen,
> And thin the boundary between.

The words are largely repetitive of what has gone before, but the truth can well bear repetition. The psalmist says, 'The Lord has established his throne in heaven, and his kingdom rules over *all*' (Ps. 103:19 RSV). That banishes from our minds any small or narrow idea of God. All parts of his dominion lie within his sight; and his dominion includes both 'this world of ours and worlds unseen'. They are all part of God's one kingdom; and the hymn finishes on a high note of praise and triumph in affirming that fact.

> One Lord one empire all secures;
> He reigns, and life and death are yours;
> Through earth and heaven one song shall ring,
> 'The Lord omnipotent is King!'

28

THINE BE THE GLORY, RISEN, CONQUERING SON
E.L. Budry, 1854–1932,
trs. R.B. Hoyle, 1875–1939

This hymn comes to us from Switzerland. Written originally in French it began, '*À toi la gloire, O Ressuscité*' and was first published in Lausanne, 1904. The English translation followed some 20 years later and like the original was set to the splendid chorus 'See the conquering hero comes' from Handel's *Judas Maccabaeus*, 1746. The hymn made a big impact when it was sung at the Jerusalem Conference in 1928 and since then has become a universal favourite.

Before looking at it we must say a word about the two men to whom we owe it, the author and the translator.

★　　★　　★

The author, Edmond Louis Budry, was born at Vevey, Switzerland, and educated at Lausanne. Here he became a licentiate in theology and philosophy of the Swiss Evangelical Free Church, a breakaway from the National Reformed Church. He served as pastor of the Free Church at Vevey from 1889 to 1924. A man with a talent for poetry, he wrote a large amount of verse, including many hymns. '*A toi la gloire*' was written in 1896, after the death of his first wife.

The English translation was made in 1923 by Richard Birch Hoyle. The son of Methodist parents, he became a Baptist minister and served his last pastorate at Kingston-upon-Thames. He was not only a man of considerable scholarship but a gifted linguist, being conversant with twelve languages. The present translation was first published in *Cantate Domino*, 1925.

These biographical notes may strike the reader as rather dull. But certainly there is nothing dull about the hymn. Its theme scarcely makes that possible. While it deals with our Lord's resurrection it is not exclusively an Easter hymn. It is sung at all times, and rightly so, since for the Christian Church it is Easter all the year round.

★   ★   ★

The two opening lines, which become the refrain, set the keynote.

> Thine be the glory, risen, conquering Son,
> Endless is the victory thou o'er death hast won.

The hymn appropriately begins on a note of worship, giving glory to the living Lord Jesus and lifting our hearts to him. It says nothing about ourselves, our feelings or our faith. We lose sight of ourselves, forget ourselves, as we magnify our Lord, 'the risen, conquering Son'.

We are taught to think of the Lord's resurrection in terms of *conquest*. Risen from the dead, he is the all-victorious Son of God; and 'endless is the victory thou o'er death hast won.' The nature of his victory is made specific. It was the complete conquest of *death* – man's last and greatest enemy. This is the reason why as Christians we do not fear death. It is a defeated foe, and God gives *us* the victory through our Lord Jesus Christ (1 Cor. 15:57). *His* victory becomes ours.

★   ★   ★

Following the refrain, the hymn continues by recalling some of the happenings of the first Easter Day, beginning with the angels and the empty tomb:

Angels in bright raiment rolled the stone away,
Kept the folded grave-clothes where the body lay.

The hymn accepts the empty tomb as historical fact, as the New Testament affirms. It was not an illusion on the part of the women. It was not something the apostles imagined or invented. Nor was it a legend of later date. It was inherent in the Gospels from the very beginning.

To suggest that the apostles preached the Resurrection as a 'spiritual' truth rather than a literal event makes nonsense of the biblical records. To argue that the women went to the wrong tomb is palpably false. And the theory that the disciples of Jesus came by night and stole his body makes not the slightest sense.

To return to the hymn. The reference to the angels rolling away the stone comes from Matthew 28:2 (AV): 'And, behold, there was a great earthquake; for an angel of the Lord descended from heaven and came and rolled back the stone.' The appearance of the angels on that resurrection morning was a visible sign of God's presence and power. It is St John's Gospel that tells of the undisturbed grave-clothes (20:4–7).

But it was not the empty tomb that finally convinced the disciples that their Lord was alive. It was his *appearances* to them that did it. The hymn goes on to speak of two of these.

Lo, Jesus meets us, risen from the tomb,
Lovingly he greets us, scatters fear and gloom;
Let the Church with gladness hymns of triumph sing,
For her Lord now liveth, death hath lost its sting.

The story of the women's return from the tomb to tell of the Lord's resurrection is related in Matthew 28:8–10:

So they departed quickly from the tomb with fear and great joy. And behold, Jesus met them and said 'All hail!' And they came up and took him by his feet and worshipped him. And Jesus said to them, 'Do not be afraid . . .'

Note how the hymn identifies *us* with the women. The risen Lord 'meets us' and 'greets us' and scatters our fear. It is a delightful touch. We read ourselves into the story and Jesus at once becomes a living reality.

★   ★   ★

The final stanza recalls another of the Lord's appearances.

> No more we doubt thee, glorious Prince of Life;
> Life is nought without thee: aid us in our strife;
> Make us more than conquerors through thy deathless
>   love;
> Bring us safe through Jordan to thy home above.

'No more we doubt thee,' as Thomas the apostle did. The familiar story is related in John 20:24–9. Thomas was not with the disciples when Jesus showed himself to them after his resurrection. But when a week later he came face to face with 'the glorious Prince of Life' his doubts were dispelled and he made the great confession of faith: 'My Lord and my God!'

The stanza ends not with praise but with prayer. We ask the risen Son of God to strengthen us in life's battle, so that through his 'deathless love' we may be more than conquerors – here and now. And what hereafter? First a safe passage 'through Jordan' (the symbol of death), and then the eternal home which the Lord has gone to prepare for us.

À toi la gloire, O Ressuscité!

29

TO GOD BE THE GLORY! GREAT THINGS HE HATH DONE
Fanny J. Crosby (Mrs F.J. van Alstyne)
1820–1915

Mrs van Alstyne is best known by her maiden name of Fanny J. Crosby. Born in South East, New York State, she had a tragic beginning to her life. When six weeks old she lost her eyesight through ignorant medical treatment. She was educated at the New York Institute for the Blind and later remained at the school as a teacher till her marriage in 1858 to Alexander van Alstyne, a blind musician.

Her flair for writing verse showed itself early in life. She published her first poems at the age of 11 and continued to write popular songs and poems in unbroken profusion. Not till mid-life was it suggested to her that instead of secular verse she should write hymns. She at once responded to the idea and devoted herself to the task till the end of her days.

Many of her hymns were used in the Moody and Sankey missions and became popular in both the USA and Britain. For a considerable time she wrote a sacred song weekly for each of three religious magazines. Her total output of verse, it is estimated, could not have been less than 9,000 pieces. Among her best-known hymns are 'Safe in the arms of Jesus', 'Rescue the perishing' and 'Blessed assurance, Jesus is mine'.

*   *   *

Strangely enough, this hymn was almost forgotten in America until recent years when it became popular in

Britain and Australia through the Billy Graham crusades. It
then found its way back to the States, where it is now a top
favourite.

The hymn has a strong and arresting start.

> To God be the glory! great things he hath done!
> So loved he the world that he gave us his Son,
> Who yielded his life an atonement for sin,
> And opened the life-gate that all may go in.

To God be the glory! The opening words are not only the key
to the hymn, they are also the key to life itself, every life, the
whole of life. The Shorter Catechism begins by asking,
'What is the chief end of man?' and it answers by affirming,
'Man's chief end is to glorify God, and enjoy him for ever.'
The hymn tells us why we should glorify God: 'great things
he hath done!'

Those great things are what the hymn is all about and it
begins with the greatest thing of all: 'God so loved the
world that he gave his only Son'; gave him to die upon the
cross, that by the laying down of his life he might reconcile
us to God and open the gate to eternal life, for all to enter
who would.

Here is the essential truth of the Christian religion: the
truth which makes the gospel good news and not good
advice. If the gospel were simply good advice it would be
about what we must do for God. But as good news it is
about what God has done for us and for our salvation. Great
things he has done indeed, and to him be the glory!

The refrain which follows each stanza begins as it should
with a call to praise.

> *Praise the Lord! Praise the Lord!*
> *Let the earth hear his voice!*
> *Praise the Lord! Praise the Lord!*
> *Let the people rejoice!*
> *O come to the Father, through Jesus the Son,*
> *And give him the glory! great things he hath done!*

'Let the earth hear his voice,' the voice of God's redeeming love. That love embraces all mankind, the whole world and everyone in it. So 'Let the people rejoice!' And not only are they to rejoice in God's love, they are invited to respond to it in faith and worship. 'O come to the Father' is the invitation; and the way to come is made plain: 'through Jesus the Son'. He himself declared, 'I am the way . . . no one comes to the Father but by me' (John 14:6). It has been rightly said that there are many ways to Christ (for Christian experience varies greatly) but there is only one way to the Father and that is 'through Jesus the Son'.

★   ★   ★

> O perfect redemption, the purchase of blood,
> To every believer the promise of God;
> The vilest offender who truly believes,
> That moment from Jesus a pardon receives.

The second stanza, in true evangelical fashion, returns to the cross. The redemption or deliverance which Christ has wrought for us and purchased by his blood is *perfect*. The word signifies that the sacrifice of the cross is sufficient and complete. It is *God's* work, done once for all, and we can neither undo it nor add anything to it.

This is what Archbishop William Temple meant when he wrote: 'All is of God. The only thing of my own which I can contribute to my own redemption is the sin from which I need to be redeemed.'

The gospel promise is 'to every believer'; that is, to everyone who trusts in Christ and his saving work, including 'the vilest offender', the worst of sinners. No one can make the excuse that he is not good enough to come to Jesus, or that he is too bad to be pardoned. For *all* there is instant salvation. It is simply a matter of believing and receiving on the sinner's part. God does the rest.

★   ★   ★

We turn to the hymn's final stanza which adds something to the great things God has done.

> Great things he hath taught us, great things he hath
>   done,
> And great our rejoicing through Jesus the Son;
> But purer and higher and greater will be
> Our wonder, our transport, when Jesus we see.

'Great things he hath taught us.' Where? Doubtless Fanny Crosby would have answered, 'In the Bible', and rightly so. Without the Bible we should know nothing of the great things God has done for us in Christ.

We need not dwell on that except to remind ourselves that as Christians we are disciples (learners) as well as believers. In fact, we are believers just because we are disciples, for our faith rests wholly on the great things God has taught us in his word. The connection between the two is plain.

Great then is our rejoicing now, in this present life. But it will be even greater still, for the best is yet to be. Fanny Crosby finished her hymn in the fashion of the day by pointing us to the heavenly glory where our praise will have its consummation and faith will turn to sight.

30

WE SING THE PRAISE OF
HIM WHO DIED
Thomas Kelly, 1769–1855

The Irish hymn-writer, Thomas Kelly, is chiefly remembered for three hymns, dealing respectively with the death, resurrection and ascension of our Lord. 'We sing the praise of him who died' is the first of these. The second is the Easter hymn, 'The Lord is risen indeed'; and the third – probably the finest of them all – 'The head that once was crowned with thorns'. Of the 750 hymns he composed the vast majority are of little worth and long forgotten; but the few that have survived are part of Ireland's rich legacy of hymnody to the Church.

His life followed an unusual course. The son of a distinguished Irish judge, he intended to follow a legal career. But at the age of 23 he was converted during the religious revival of 1792, and dedicating his life to the Lord's service he was ordained to the ministry of the Church of Ireland. However he soon fell foul of the Archbishop of Dublin, who disapproved of his 'Methodistical' preaching and barred him from church pulpits.

Kelly was not a man to be daunted by this, so parting company with the archbishop and the Irish Church he turned Dissenter. Having ample means he built chapels in various places where he and his friends were free to preach. He was renowned throughout Ireland for his preaching, but he was equally renowned for his great benevolence. He was a friend of every good cause, and during the grim years of famine gave generous help to the poverty-stricken people.

★   ★   ★

'We sing the praise of him who died' was published in 1815 and headed: 'God forbid that I should glory, save in the cross of our Lord Jesus Christ.' That was also the text that inspired Isaac Watts's 'When I survey the wondrous cross' a century before. The two hymns have much in common and both turn our eyes in the same direction.

> We sing the praise of him who died,
>> Of him who died upon the cross;
> The sinner's hope let men deride,
>> For this we count the world but loss.

Thomas Kelly, like the apostle, gloried in the cross. But in his hymn he is praising not the cross itself but 'him who died upon the cross'. He gloried in the cross only because it was the cross of Jesus. For him the cross had no value or merit apart from the Crucified.

Again, Kelly gloried in the cross because he recognised in the Crucified 'the sinner's hope', the sinner's only hope of salvation – let men deride or deny it as they will. He was not concerned about the world's opinion, meaning the godless world. 'For this we count the world but loss.'

These words are a further reference to St Paul's words in Galatians 6 about the cross of Jesus as the one 'by which the world has been crucified to me, and I to the world' (v. 14). The death of the Son of God establishes a new relationship between the believer and the world, the world that rejected and crucified his Lord.

The next stanza gives a new glimpse of the glory of the cross.

> Inscribed upon the cross we see
>> In shining letters 'God is Love';
> He bears our sins upon the tree,
>> He brings us pardon from above.

There is a strikingly imaginative touch in the opening lines. The Gospels tell us that over the Cross was written, 'This is

Jesus the king of the Jews'. They were intended to be words of condemnation. But to the eye of faith they read quite differently. They are transfigured into shining letters of gold and read 'God is Love' – the message of salvation.

In the crucified Redeemer we see a glowing revelation of what God is, and more than that, of what he has done for us. 'God shows his love for us in that while we were yet sinners Christ died for us' (Rom. 5:8 RSV). It was indeed *for us* he died: 'He bears *our* sins upon the tree'. His death was no mere example or martyrdom. It was a vicarious sacrifice. The Lord laid on him the iniquity of us all (Isa. 53:6). And it was his grace that did it: 'He brings us mercy from above.'

★   ★   ★

The stanzas that follow might be headed 'The Cross in Christian experience'.

> The cross! it takes our guilt away,
>   It holds the fainting spirit up;
> It cheers with hope the gloomy day,
>   And sweetens every bitter cup.

Each of the four lines makes a separate point.

First, the cross releases us from our guilty fears and brings us the peace of sins forgiven.

Next, it supports us in times of weakness, especially in the hour of temptation.

Again, it cheers us in our dark hours by kindling hope in our hearts.

And last, it consoles us amid life's bitter things, its pains, sorrows and disappointments.

All this makes clear that the cross is not just a piece of theology but a truth that impinges directly on our everyday life. And more follows on the same lines.

> It makes the coward spirit brave,
>   And nerves the feeble arm for fight;

> It takes its terror from the grave,
>   And gilds the bed of death with light.

This stanza relates the cross to the realities of life and death, and first to life. We know only too well 'the coward spirit' in us all and 'the feeble arm' of the flesh. Where shall we find the courage and strength we need? By 'looking unto Jesus': the one who for our sake 'endured the cross, despising the shame, and is now seated at the right hand of God' (Heb. 12:2 RSV).

The cross gives us courage to die as well as to live. 'It takes its terror from the grave,' and it does that because by his death Christ has vanquished death and opened to us the gate of everlasting life. And so the hymn continues:

> The balm of life, the cure of woe,
>   The measure and the pledge of love,
> The sinner's refuge here below,
>   The angels' theme in heaven above.

In general these words sum up all that has gone before. Their most important feature is the return to the theme of the love of God, of which the cross is both the measure and the pledge. The *measure*, though in fact it is infinite and therefore immeasurable. And the *pledge*, the guarantee that his love is real, unchangeable, and enfolds us all. No wonder the angels sing about it in heaven!

31

WHEN MORNING GILDS THE SKIES
Anonymous, nineteenth century,
trs. Edward Caswall, 1814–78

What a fine tune it was that Sir Joseph Barnby wrote for this hymn in *Hymns Ancient and Modern*, 1868! He called it *Laudes Domini* ('Praise to the Lord') and it is still to be found in most hymn-books. Another tune is available, but the original remains the popular choice. It splendidly catches the spirit of the words and has the power to lift the heart.

The hymn is anonymous, so it is not possible to write about the author. Instead, I will say something about the composer of the tune.

Joseph Barnby (1838–96) was one of the leading church musicians of the Victorian era. He began his career as organist of several London churches and later won renown for his outstanding gifts as a choirmaster. His annual performances of Bach's Passion music at St Anne's, Soho, became a feature of the musical life of London. He was conductor of the Royal Choral Society and in 1892 was knighted and appointed principal of the Guildhall School of Music.

He wrote vast quantities of church music, including more than 200 hymn tunes. Many of these were widely used in his lifetime, but their popularity diminished in the present century and other tunes took their place. However his *Laudes Domini* remains, and we are grateful for it whenever we sing 'When morning gilds the skies'.

*   *   *

The hymn is of German origin and dates from 1828. The English translation is the work of Edward Caswall, a former Anglican priest who entered the Roman Catholic Church in 1850 and translated many of the medieval Latin hymns. His translation of this German hymn in its final form consisted of fourteen stanzas. Varied selections and arrangements of these appear in the hymn-books. We shall look at half a dozen which make a suitable hymn of praise.

The structure of the hymn is very simple. Running all through it is the refrain 'May Jesus Christ be praised!' interspersed with a series of couplets which provide the substance of the work.

> When morning gilds the skies,
> My heart awaking cries,
>   'May Jesus Christ be praised!'
> Alike at work and prayer
> To Jesus I repair:
>   'May Jesus Christ be praised!'

The opening line gives the impression that this is a morning hymn, but the work as a whole dispels that illusion. It is a hymn for any hour of the day, for the evening as much as for the morning.

To begin with, we are to praise Christ at the break of day, with our hearts wide awake as well as our bodies. And then, through the hours of the day, we are to continue our praise, 'alike at work and prayer'. Our work should not hinder our prayer, and our prayer certainly will not hinder our work. If our work is truly offered to God for his glory it becomes part of our prayer life; and both work and prayer are sanctified by praise.

The day is finished and the night draws near. What then?

> Be this, when day is past,
> Of all my thoughts the last,
>   'May Jesus Christ be praised!'

> The night becomes as day
> When from the heart we say,
>   'May Jesus Christ be praised!'

We retire to bed and prepare for the night. As we do so our last thoughts should be to praise Christ for the day he has given us and also for the sleep he will give us in the coming night. Sound sleep is one of God's priceless gifts to weary bodies and minds. And as the darkness envelops us we have no cause to fear, for with God day and night are both alike. 'Even the darkness is not dark to thee; the night is bright as the day' (Ps. 139:12 RSV).

★   ★   ★

Not all our days flow peacefully and happily. Some are shadowed by grief, others disturbed by evil thoughts.

> Does sadness fill my mind?
> A solace here I find,
>   'May Jesus Christ be praised!'
> When evil thoughts molest,
> With this I shield my breast,
>   'May Jesus Christ be praised!'

There are many things in life to make us sad, such as illness or bereavement, the wrongs done by others and the terrible happenings in the world around. How then do we find solace in the refrain, 'May Jesus Christ be praised'? Perhaps because to sing such words not only lifts us above our sadness but also turns our thoughts from ourselves to him who is the source of all true consolation and strength.

And then there are those evil thoughts which molest us at times. They cannot always be avoided, but we need not harbour them. We can drive them out of our hearts in the name of our victorious Saviour as we give him praise.

The hymn continues in another strain.

> To God the Word on high
> The hosts of angels cry,
>   'May Jesus Christ be praised!'
> Let mortals too upraise
> Their voice in hymns of praise:
>   'May Jesus Christ be praised!'

The thought here is that heaven and earth combine in praising Christ, 'God the Word on high', the Word once made flesh for us, now exalted to the right hand of the Father. To him the angelic hosts cry, 'May Jesus Christ be praised!' And we mere mortals on earth, as though not to be outdone by them, lift up our voices and echo their song. The music of heaven and earth is one.

> Let earth's wide circle round
> In joyful notes resound:
>   'May Jesus Christ be praised!'
> Let air and sea and sky
> In depth to height reply,
>   'May Jesus Christ be praised!'

The call here is to universal praise. In joyful notes the whole earth is to resound with the praises of Jesus, for he is Lord of all, and 'air and sea and sky' are to join in the same song. As in the book of Psalms, the world of nature is summoned to praise its Creator.

*   *   *

The final stanza, like the earlier ones, is personal in character:

> Be this while life is mine
> My canticle divine:
>   'May Jesus Christ be praised!'

> Be this the eternal song
> Through all the ages long,
> 'May Jesus Christ be praised!'

Angels in heaven, mortals on earth, the whole world of creation, sing their praises to Jesus. But that is not all. Each of us individually must join in this great galaxy of praise. 'Be this while *life* is mine . . .' the hymn says. It is mine now. It will not be mine for ever in this world. Let me then use it: not simply to *sing* the Saviour's praise, but to show it forth in my life every day I live.

32

YE SERVANTS OF GOD, YOUR MASTER PROCLAIM
Charles Wesley, 1707–88

Charles Wesley again, the third of his hymns in this book (see Chapters 4 and 24). We could hardly have found a finer one with which to finish our hymns of praise. It pulsates with praise and joy from beginning to end. Yet Wesley published it in 1744 in a pamphlet entitled *Hymns for Times of Trouble and Persecution* and it is the first of several hymns 'to be sung in time of tumult'.

That must seem rather odd, for the hymn as we have it contains no hint of tumult or trouble. The explanation is that two of the original stanzas are missing, so that what was written as a sort of battle-song now becomes a splendid Te Deum, extolling the greatness of God and the glories of Christ.

The omitted stanzas at once clarify the matter.

> The waves of the sea have lift up their voice,
> Sore troubled that we in Jesus rejoice;
> The floods, they are roaring, but Jesus is here,
> While we are adoring he always is near.

> Men, devils engage, the billows arise,
> And horribly rage, and threaten the skies;
> Their fury shall never our steadfastness shock,
> The weakest believer is built on a rock.

In their early days the Wesleys and the Methodist people were subject to much persecution, as their *Journals* record.

In all parts of the country the preachers and their converts were constantly assaulted and abused, mobbed and stoned. And this was done with the connivance and encouragement of the clergy and 'chief gentlemen' of the place. We can readily picture the small but heroic Methodist bands facing the fury of their persecutors with Wesley's rousing and triumphant songs 'in time of tumult' upon their lips.

★   ★   ★

We now look at the four stanzas of the hymn which we have in our hymn-books. Perhaps their dominant note is the sovereignty of God, the assurance that in all life's circumstances 'the Lord reigneth'.

> Ye servants of God, your Master proclaim,
> And publish abroad his wonderful name:
> The name all-victorious of Jesus extol,
> His kingdom is glorious, and rules over all.

You will note that the words here are addressed not to God but to the 'servants of God'. There is no doubt as to which of God's servants Wesley had specially in mind.

You will note, too, that the hymn begins with a call not to praise but to proclamation. The persecuted Methodists are to 'publish abroad' their Master's wonderful name. They are not to be silenced or intimidated by their oppressors. In all circumstances they are to maintain a faithful witness to Jesus in word and song.

With proclamation goes praise: 'The name all-victorious of Jesus extol'. Proclamation is addressed to men, praise to God. Proclamation is part of our witness, praise of our worship. They are perfect partners. Here we praise Jesus as conqueror and king. The hymn continues in the same strain.

> God ruleth on high, almighty to save,
> And still he is nigh: his presence we have;
> The great congregation his triumph shall sing,
> Ascribing salvation to Jesus our King.

There is a lot of comfort to be derived from the opening lines. First, because the Lord 'ruleth on high' we know that he has the whole human situation in his hands, our own lives included. We are not the victims of blind chance. God is Almighty, which means that nothing can happen without his permission.

The other comfort is that though transcendent he is not a remote or absent deity. 'Still he is nigh' – always, everywhere. We do not have to seek his presence. 'His presence we *have*', here and now. All that is needed on our part is to be aware of it, to practise it, cultivate it, enjoy it, so that it becomes a spiritual reality.

'The great congregation his triumph shall sing'. What did Wesley mean by the great congregation? At that time the congregations in the Methodist meeting-places were small. On the other hand the open-air congregations that gathered to hear the Wesleys preach were vast. But there is another possibility. The 'great congregation' may refer to the Church in heaven, as in the next stanza, and this makes good sense.

★　　★　　★

> Salvation to God, who sits on the throne!
> Let all cry aloud, and honour the Son;
> The praises of Jesus the angels proclaim,
> Fall down on their faces, and worship the Lamb.

We are transported to heaven where St John sees a vision of the throne of God surrounded by a great multitude crying out with a loud voice, 'Salvation belongs to our God who sits upon the throne and to the Lamb!' (Rev. 7:9, 10 RSV).

The praises here seem to be those of redeemed mankind, for they come 'from every nation, from all tribes and peoples and tongues' (v. 9).

But the praises of Jesus are also sung by the angels. Wesley now takes us to another passage of the same book:

> Then I looked and heard . . . the voice of many angels, numbering myriads of myriads and thousands of thousands, saying with a loud voice, 'Worthy is the Lamb who was slain to receive power and wealth and wisdom and might and honour and glory and blessing!' (5:11 RSV).

The courts of heaven ring with the unceasing praise of Jesus from men and angels. But what of ourselves here on earth?

> Then let us adore, and give him his right;
> All glory and power, all wisdom and might,
> All honour and blessing, with angels above,
> And thanks never ceasing, and infinite love.

'Then let *us* adore'. This is where we come in. We have been spectators before. Now we become worshippers and adore the Lamb. The word adore comes from the Latin *ad orare*, which means literally to pray. But that meaning has long been left behind. To adore, as the dictionary says, is to love, to worship or revere intensely, and that is what the hymn is calling us to do.

'And give him his *right*' – another significant word. In praising the Lord we are giving him what is rightfully his. We are rendering him, as one of the Psalms says, the honour *due* to his name; it is something we *owe* him. The debt is ours because of our creation. It is the Lord who made us and we are his. But more, much more, the debt is ours because of our redemption. We have been bought at a price.

The praise we thus owe him is spelt out in the magnificent string of words which concludes the hymn, derived from

Revelation 7:12. All that is his by right. And something else as well, more important than any words: the devotion of our hearts and the dedication of our lives.

INDEX OF AUTHORS AND TRANSLATORS